The HAPPINESS PRACTICE

The HAPPINESS PRACTICE

A Guide to WHAT MATTERS MOST

Victor Mena

COPYRIGHT © 2023 VICTOR F. MENA
All rights reserved.

THE HAPPINESS PRACTICE

A Guide to What Matters Most

ISBN	978-1-5445-3952-2	*Paperback*
	978-1-5445-3953-9	*Ebook*
	978-1-5445-3954-6	*Audiobook*

To my family

CONTENTS

Introduction — 1

Chapter 1
HAPPINESS IS A PRACTICE — 5

Chapter 2
THE PRISON OF OUR PAST — 23

Chapter 3
PERSPECTIVE IS PARAMOUNT — 45

Chapter 4
THE POWER OF IDEAS — 65

Chapter 5
BLACK SWANS — 85

Chapter 6
YOUR HAPPINESS ROADMAP — 105

Chapter 7
BE YOUR OWN BEST FRIEND — 145

Conclusion — 165

Bibliography — 167

About the Author — 175

INTRODUCTION

> Happiness is the meaning and the purpose of life,
> the whole aim, and end of human existence.
> **—ARISTOTLE, PHILOSOPHER**

My two younger brothers and I shared a room for most of our childhood. We sometimes stayed up at night talking and watching horror movies. Our parents didn't know. Even though we bent the rules a little bit, those late nights with my brothers are some of my most cherished memories.

Happiness came easy to me then. Little did I know that decades later, I would struggle with lighting that spark again.

The spark sputtered and dimmed in my mid-thirties, after my business partner and mentor died unexpectedly in 2013. At the time, my mom was recovering from brain cancer, and my brother was battling alcoholism while I was adjusting to life as a newlywed. I was stretched thin, both personally and professionally. I grappled with grief while simultaneously trying to sort out the implications for our company and avoid being dragged into an ugly legal fight over my business partner's inheritance. I lay awake at night worrying. I was so overwhelmed with the seemingly insurmountable challenges that I couldn't focus or make meaningful progress in any aspect of my life.

Deep-seated doubts, depression, anxiety, grief, and questions about life's purpose arise in most of us at one point or another. Then we must decide what to do—ignore the anger, sadness, and disappointment or reckon with our feelings and reflect on where we're headed. I had a good life—a loving family, an interesting job, a comfortable home, and good friends. Why was I depressed?

Maybe you've felt the same, even if you have a different background and life experiences. Perhaps, like me, you feel guilty for feeling bad, yet it doesn't change how unhappy and restless you are. Maybe you've also struggled with a constant low level of frustration and a vague sense that something was missing but didn't know exactly what.

Since I had no clue what was wrong with me, how could I figure out what to do to move forward or advance in any way? But I also knew I couldn't stay where I was, constantly complaining about my life and making everyone around me miserable. I didn't like the grouchy, ill-tempered, unproductive human I was becoming. I was getting worried about damaging my relationships and losing my livelihood.

Considering what I truly wanted out of my life, the answer came to me clearly and simply: I wanted to be happy above all else. I didn't want to be a kid again, but I did want to reclaim the way I used to find happiness in simple things. I wanted to savor moments shared with loved ones and treasure life's small delights and surprises. I needed to focus my attention on the now, rather than ruminating on the past or worrying about the future. Getting clear on who I wanted to be and what I wanted my life to look like didn't fix anything overnight, but it did give me the drive to start looking for solutions.

I'm an industrial engineer turned real estate fund manager, not a psychologist, so I approached this challenge like I approached engineering problems at work. I learned as much as possible, then brainstormed potential solutions, and finally, applied them to my own life to see if the theory worked in practice. It was a process of trial and error. This book you hold in your hands is a collection of my lab notes about what I've learned along the way.

This book is neither a stuffy academic tome nor a fluffy five-steps-to-happiness listicle. It's not a magic bullet but a practical guide that distills decades of academic research and personal experience into straightforward concepts you can apply to your life today. I hope this book will be a resource for you to claim whatever happiness you can.

Some people say you have to hit rock bottom to find the will to change and sink as low as possible to see the only way is up. I don't believe that. We can change whenever we decide to. There is no bottom, no hole to crawl out of. These were just theoretical constructs, ideas that kept me immobile and stuck. I could see no point in waiting until I'd lost my job and my family to make changes.

Many constraints and circumstances affect our happiness, including biological, environmental, and systemic conditions beyond our control. If you think you might suffer from a mental health condition that can affect your happiness, such as anxiety and depression, I encourage you to seek professional help. Practicing happiness does not mean ignoring or minimizing the pain life brings. Don't let toxic positivity shame you into sucking it up or plastering a fake smile on your face.

The tools I share with you in this book will not magically perfect your life, but they can drastically change your perspective. Unlearning years of faulty thinking and unhealthy behaviors doesn't happen overnight. There is no switch to flip. But with time and effort, you will see a dramatic change in how you think, feel, and interact with people.

This book will give you a framework with resources and options you can customize to apply to your own life, in your own way, and on your own timeline. The hands-on exercises in each chapter allow you to practice the concepts. They will teach you to identify distorted thinking, reframe skewed perspectives, understand your emotions, improve decision making, and gain more peace, clarity, and happiness.

Regardless of what life throws at you, no matter how dire your situation may seem, there is always something you have control over. In *Man's Search for Meaning*, Viktor E. Frankl explains, "Everything can be taken from a man but one thing: the last of the human freedoms—to choose one's attitude in any given set of circumstances, to choose one's own way."[1]

Every day you can choose to be as happy as possible. I hope that whatever limitations on your happiness you deal with, this book will encourage you to start a daily happiness practice to increase the bright spots in your days.

---

1 Frankl, *Man's Search*, 75.

Chapter 1
HAPPINESS IS A PRACTICE

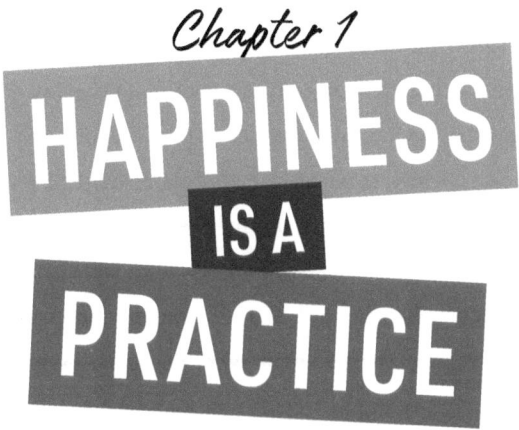

> God, grant me the serenity to accept the things I cannot change, courage to change the things I can, and wisdom to know the difference.
> **—REINHOLD NIEBUHR, AUTHOR**

"Why don't you look for a different job?" I asked Arjun, the teenage errand boy I had struck up a conversation with outside a Mumbai craft store while waiting for my wife to buy souvenirs.

"I'm happy with my work." He smiled.

My wife, Cynthia, and I had been on a tour of the beautiful city of Mumbai earlier in the day, soaking in its rich color and culture. We toured a multibillion-dollar building that housed six members of one of India's wealthiest families, which stood three blocks away from a communal washing place for the city's poorest inhabitants. People come to wash their clothes in the river, which is heavily polluted with garbage and raw sewage. The sopping wet garments are laid out on the dirt to be baked dry in the sun. Seeing this jarring contrast between the richest and poorest within a few blocks of the city, I wondered why there wasn't more civil unrest or even war.

To be sure, similar levels of inequality had led to severe and prolonged conflict in many other parts of the world. Why not India? In 2021, India's average per capita income was roughly 86,659 rupees, which translates to approximately $1,114 annually or $3.10 a day.[2] Arjun's entire family lived on less than $4 a day, and many other families had to make do with less than $2. As an errand boy, he looked for work on the crowded squares where vendors and foreigners milled about every day, offering his services to deliver packages, food, or drinks back and forth between tourists and their hotels. He worked long hours crisscrossing the city on his bike. He spoke English surprisingly well, and the insights he shared stuck with me.

Arjun explained that his Hindu beliefs centering on reincarnation allowed him to be content, even happy, with his life. He said suffering is part of life, and with every death and rebirth, the cycle would repeat until he reached enlightenment.

There are, of course, many people of many different religions and faith traditions whose beliefs in the afterlife or reincarnation give them a sense of purpose and hope that can translate to increased happiness in daily life. However, even without religious or spiritual beliefs, the idea that suffering is simply a fact of life that we all need to contend with can be a powerful tool in our quest for more happiness. Pain and suffering will inevitably come for all of us. How will we respond? Will we try to escape it or spend our energy asking *why me?*

What if, just like Arjun, we accepted pain and suffering as a

---

2 Statista, "Income across India 2011 to 2021."

natural part of life and decided to be as happy as possible anyway? What if we viewed happiness less as an elusive goal we could only reach if external circumstances aligned and more as an inner practice we could commit to every single day?

> **WHAT ARE THE BENEFITS OF VIEWING HAPPINESS AS A PRACTICE?**
> - You will see happiness as an ongoing process rather than a destination.
> - You will feel empowered to take your life into your own hands.
> - You will be inspired to make impactful change where possible.
> - You will determine what happiness means to you personally.

According to the *Oxford English Dictionary*, happiness is a "state of pleasurable contentment of mind." Although we may disagree on what exactly happiness means for each of us, how it can be attained has proved to be even more of a mystery. In this chapter, we'll talk about the difference between two forms of happiness and whether our practice should be focused internally or externally. We'll discuss whether money can truly buy happiness and how living in the real world versus in cyberspace might impact our practice. Finally, I'll share with you the foundation for my own happiness practice and invite you to try it out for yourself.

DAILY HAPPINESS VERSUS LIFE SATISFACTION

We want to strengthen and enhance aspects of our lives that result in more joy, surprise, delight, and laughter today in order to create a meaningful and interesting life we can look back on with satisfaction. Researchers Daniel Kahneman and Angus Deaton first made this distinction between two different types of happiness: positive daily emotions and overall life satisfaction. Ideally, we want our daily practice to impact both types of happiness.

Think back to celebrating Christmas or any other significant holiday or special occasion with your family when you were a child. Do you recall running out of your bedroom on Christmas morning to catch your first glimpse of the tree all lit up, with shiny presents underneath, and soft Christmas music playing in the background? Perhaps you felt happy, even ecstatic. But shortly after, did you feel a letdown once all the gifts were unwrapped and you sat amid a pile of cardboard, realizing the event you'd anticipated for months was over, and now you'd have to wait another year for Christmas to roll around again?

However, thinking back on holidays with your family, you'll likely have overwhelmingly fond memories of the traditions, special foods, celebrations, and activities. You may re-create some of them in your own family today. Certain smells, tastes, or songs might bring back pleasant memories and a sense of overall satisfaction with your childhood or gratitude for the family you grew up in. The point is that our feelings of happiness in the moment can change quickly and are not necessarily a one-to-one representation of how happy recalling these events will make us years or decades from now.

These two distinct types of happiness, "in the moment" and "looking back," both affect us, but our perspective on leveraging each of them is skewed. On the one hand, we tend to think achieving goals and accolades will give us happiness in the moment, which they often don't. However, they frequently do add to our overall life satisfaction. On the other hand, we believe family and friends are essential for a happy and successful life. Still, we don't prioritize spending quality time together, despite the fact that doing so is one of the strongest predictors of daily happiness. In this book, we'll talk about how to craft a happiness practice that impacts both your daily and long-term happiness and satisfaction.

In Western cultures, we tend to view happiness as a direct result of material wealth and external achievement rather than as an active, internal practice. That's one reason we're so often stunned by people like Arjun, who live in poverty but seem much happier than us.

CAN MONEY BUY HAPPINESS?

The World Bank estimates that, in 2020, 9.2 percent of the world's population lived in extreme poverty on less than $1.90 a day.[3] These numbers are difficult to comprehend because they translate to 689 million people, more than twice the US population. Living in comparative wealth and luxury makes it almost impossible to grasp how different our lives are economically from these hundreds of millions of people. And yet, we are not necessarily happier than they are.

You may be familiar with the oft-cited study by Israeli American psychologist Daniel Kahneman showing that happiness increases as our income grows but only up to a certain point. Once we hit about $75,000 a year, money brings diminishing returns when it comes to daily happiness and well-being.[4] However, as we've discussed, Kahneman distinguishes between two ways to measure happiness and how they impact the study results. One measure

---

[3] Castaneda Aguilar et al., "September 2020 Global Poverty Update."
[4] Kahneman and Deaton, "High Income Improves Life," 16490–16492.

is overall life evaluation, and the second is emotional well-being. The first asked study participants to contemplate their life as a whole and judge whether this was the best or worst life they could imagine for themselves. The second asked them to consider their daily emotions, recent positive experiences, feelings of joy and happiness, laughter, and well-being.

The study's results are a bit more nuanced than sometimes reported. Kahneman states that life evaluation continues to increase with income, but daily happiness and emotional well-being stalls beyond $75,000 a year (or $90,000 when adjusted for inflation). Kahneman and his fellow study collaborator Angus Deaton concluded that "high income buys life satisfaction but not happiness, and low income is associated both with low life evaluation and low emotional well-being."

It makes sense that if money can buy more basic necessities and safety, it significantly impacts our happiness. Once our basic needs are met, money no longer adds much to our daily happiness, although it continues to make us more satisfied with our lives overall.

I'm guessing 99.99 percent of people reading this book are in a better economic position than Arjun, yet almost all are significantly less happy. Why? As we'll discuss in the upcoming chapters, although material wealth can certainly reduce suffering and increase our happiness up to a certain point, many other factors are also at play. Essentially, our momentary happiness and overall life satisfaction are always a snapshot and a mosaic of many interacting forces, circumstances, and actions. Many are outside of our control, and the ones that aren't, require consistent daily attention and energy.

THE INTERNAL FOCUS OF OUR HAPPINESS PRACTICE

Some people may argue that instead of cultivating an internal daily practice, they would be much happier if they reached certain intermediate or long-term life goals. Maybe that means getting a better job or nicer car, losing those last ten pounds, finding a partner, having a baby, or taking a dream vacation. But once we reach the elusive destination we were striving toward or acquire the material item we wanted so badly, we often replace that desire with something new. We think we will be satisfied once we achieve a goal, but instead, we feel let down.

In his book *Happier*, author Tal Ben-Shahar calls this phenomenon the "arrival fallacy."[5] Reaching goals, having a successful career, or creating a family all can lead to enhancing our overall life satisfaction, the kind of happiness Kahneman explained comes from looking back on a life that matches what we expected or desired. Although this constant striving helps us progress, it rarely adds to our daily happiness.

Therefore, we'll focus on an internal practice rather than trying to gain happiness through reaching external objectives. This doesn't mean we won't talk about goals and work and relationships. I don't believe in accepting a stoic philosophy where we merely detach from everything and everyone to achieve a state of calm and neutrality. There are undoubtedly external circumstances that impact our happiness. Instead of dismissing them, there are important lessons to be learned that can and should inform our next steps. Centering our practice internally is more about focusing on the aspects of life we can control, whether that's

---

5 Ben-Shahar, *Happier*, 25.

our thoughts and perspectives, our goal-setting approach, or the time and energy we allot for the priorities in our lives.

Currently, so many of the ideas surrounding happiness focus on external validation, status symbols, and markers of supposed happiness, rather than fully experiencing our lives. We go to the most instagrammable spots on our vacation to take the perfect picture to impress our followers, instead of getting lost in the streets of a new city, trying different foods, interacting with locals, and admiring the architecture. We post filtered or straight-up fake images to appear wealthier, better looking, more successful, and happier than we are. We show the highlight reel of our lives and hide the reality, the mess, the struggle, the hard times.

We buy things we don't need with money we haven't earned to impress people we don't like. This pithy statement on our human need to compare ourselves to others has no clear attribution, but it hits the core of social comparison. Why do we focus on achieving status, fame, and material items to keep up, even though none of those things make us happier in the long term?

The problem is much older than social media, but we see the negative impact of social comparison and FOMO (fear of missing out) play out at heightened intensity on the internet. Although attempting to improve our social status is part of being human, our culture's obsession with social media now allows us to compare our lives not only to our neighbors but to millions of strangers as well. Social media in and of itself is not the issue. It's how we use it that can affect our happiness positively or negatively. I have found gratitude to be a remarkable counterweight to an obsessive external focus. Especially when struggling with social comparison, practicing gratitude helps me keep a balanced view of my life.

GRATITUDE AS THE FOUNDATION OF A HAPPINESS PRACTICE

Constant comparison can result in our tendency to focus on the difficulties in our lives rather than the areas that could inspire gratitude. We shouldn't ignore our problems or issues, but it's worth examining whether we're putting disproportionate focus and attention on our lack rather than our abundance. We often take for granted what we have and the people we love. The old adage that *we don't know what we got till it's gone* rings true. It takes conscious effort to pay attention to all the beauty already in our lives right now, but it's a surefire way to increase our happiness.

One of the most foundational practices to increase happiness is incorporating gratitude into our daily lives. In 2003, Emmons and McCullough's study in the *Journal of Personality and Social Psychology* found that a ten-week gratitude practice correlated with enhanced well-being, specifically positive affect—our tendency to experience positive emotions and interact with others and life's challenges in a constructive way.[6] Unsurprisingly, another study showed that gratitude is good for our romantic relationships because it increases feelings of mutual appreciation, facilitates a higher willingness to respond to each other's needs, and results in an increased likelihood to maintain long-term close bonds.[7]

There are plenty of different gratitude practices with varying approaches, verbal or written, short or long, focused on specific aspects of our lives. The exercise I suggest below is one for you to try out, but feel free to adapt it to your life. The specific approach is less important than the effort to practice gratitude each day.

---

6 Emmons and McCullough, "Blessings versus Burdens," 377–389.
7 Gordon et al., "To Have," 270.

EXERCISE

Keep a Gratitude Journal for One Week

Grab a notebook, journal, or piece of paper. For the next seven days, write down five things you are grateful for at the end of each day.

The trick is to make these items specific to the day. Rather than writing "I'm grateful for my family," note a particular interaction you are thankful for. For example, "I'm grateful for spending quality time with my daughter today when we went to the park, and she trusted me enough to tell me about a fight with her best friend."

Mix it up between small things, like a stranger smiling at you on the subway, and big things, like landing a promotion. Think beyond the usual topics of family, friends, and health. There are many things to be grateful for that don't always make our top priority list. What are you thankful for about the place you live? The clean air, the community events, the reliable public transportation, the great weather? What about all the people in your life, aside from primary relationships, who make your day better—the teacher who encourages your dyslexic son, the bank teller who remembers your name, or the neighbor who shovels your sidewalk? Are you grateful for your body? No, not for how it looks but for how it helps you experience life. Are you thankful for how the sun feels on your face after a long winter, the butterflies in your stomach the morning of your wedding, or the warm, heavy weight of a sleeping child in your arms?

As you record the things you're grateful for, keep these helpful tips in mind:

- Be specific.
- Pay attention to both the small and big joys.
- Look beyond the ordinary.

And after the week is over, keep going if it makes you happy.

Happiness is based on complex facets, but our response to any given situation matters greatly regardless of circumstances. We often think our happiness is related to how much we have, how successful we are, and our perceived status compared to our neighbors. Although having our basic needs met certainly improves life satisfaction, social comparison can quickly ruin any happiness gains we've achieved.

Arjun is a perfect example that we can be happy even if our environment tempts us to continually compare our lives to those of our neighbors. Practicing gratitude can shift our focus to all the good in our lives, rather than worrying about how we stack up against millions of other people. Gratitude also helps us stay grounded in our real lives and relationships rather than escaping into aspirational but fake online identities.

CAN SOCIAL MEDIA BE A POSITIVE PART OF YOUR HAPPINESS PRACTICE?

Social media is a powerful tool with positive or negative impacts depending on how we use it. A 2021 study showed that using social media for communication with like-minded people and groups can make us feel less lonely and satisfy our individual needs for social connection and relationships.[8] Especially during the pandemic, online connections with our loved ones and a feeling of community with perfect strangers helped many of us see at least a glimpse of that belonging we'd typically experience in face-to-face interactions.

Even when there is not a pandemic keeping friends and families apart, social media fills a vital gap for connection in

---

8 Graciyal and Viswam, "Happiness or Pleasure," 103.

long-distance relationships. Further, social media offers an online gathering place where people can share their passions, talents, and interests or participate in self-help groups for nearly every illness, addiction, or hardship.

However, if we use social media to gain status, fame, followers, and likes, we tend to compare ourselves to others and slip into FOMO. Both social comparison and FOMO significantly decrease our subjective happiness. A 2021 study in the *Journal of Happiness Studies* by Wirtz et al. explains that social comparison on social media results in increased negative affect, meaning people experience more feelings of anger, guilt, fear, and contempt.[9] Social media apps like TikTok, Snapchat, Instagram, and Facebook, in particular, have become a source of FOMO for users, which can lead to a rise in loneliness and depression, according to a 2018 study by Melissa Hunt and Rachel Marx published in the *Journal of Social and Clinical Psychology*.[10]

Social media can even become an addiction. Hunt and Marx caution parents that "95 percent of United States adolescents had access to a smartphone, and 45 percent said they were online 'almost constantly' to the detriment of spending time with offline activities, such as healthy sleep, exercise, social interactions, and attending religious services compared to those who do not spend so much time in a virtual reality."

In a review of several studies about youth and social media use, Manago and Vaughn explain that social media provides both "new opportunities and risks for happiness in the journey to adulthood," citing "increased convenience for cultivating closeness with friends and enhanced access to social information and

---

9 Wirtz et al., "Social Media Subjective Well-Being," 1673-1691.
10 Hunt et al., "No More FOMO," 763-764.

social capital, which lend themselves to forms of social support." The risks uncovered in this study included that young people face the "allure of transient pleasures of instant gratification friendship and social snacking, increased demands to negotiate promotional self-presentations broadcasted by shallow networks of contacts, and the challenge to cultivate happiness in a social world that seems to increasingly define self-worth and life satisfaction based on image, success, and popularity."[11]

Wonder if you or your child are headed toward developing a phone addiction? Ask yourself or your teen if you/they feel restless when the phones are out of reach. Pay attention to how often you have the urge to pick up your phone throughout the day. Use an app like Screen Time to see how much time you spend on your phone compared to other activities. Take note of how often you forgo sleep because you can't stop scrolling, aren't present for a conversation because you're checking notifications, or prefer texting over spending time with a friend in person. It's difficult for grown-ups to make healthy decisions about phone and social media use, and it's even more challenging for our children. Kids and teenagers whose brains are still actively developing are less emotionally mature and thus more susceptible to the allure of social media apps. They need our guidance and, most importantly, our example.

Social media isn't going anywhere, and neither are its impacts on our mental health and happiness. We must find a reasonable balance. We need to have discussions with our partners, be mindful of our own social media use, and model healthy behavior to our children.

According to MIT Professor Sinan Aral, "Social media is rewiring

---

[11] Manago and Vaughn, "Social Media, Friendship, and Happiness," abstract.

the central nervous system of humanity in real time," and many of the impacts are yet to be seen.[12] If we notice that the endless highlight reels of social media celebrities dampen our satisfaction and happiness with our own lives, we don't need to wait for a study to tell us it's okay to log off. We can make that choice at any time. Think of this book as an invitation to learn about the scientific evidence, become more self-aware, experiment, and see for yourself what makes the biggest impact on your happiness.

Although I don't propose cutting social media from your life, being very honest with yourself about your use is the first step in determining whether social media adds to or diminishes your happiness. If you're unsure, you can experiment and see what happens. Wirtz and his colleagues learned in their study that "over 10 days, greater everyday use of social media resulted in lower subjective well-being...In evaluating why use of social media adversely impacted subjective well-being, social comparison was a strong predictor. Specifically, the more that participants reported comparing themselves to others while using social media, the less subjective well-being they subsequently experienced. In contrast, traditional, offline social interactions exerted the opposite (beneficial) effect on happiness: increasing positive affect and decreasing negative affect."[13]

In other words, if you're prone to using social media to compare yourself to others, your happiness may increase the less time you spend on the platforms. If you tend toward social comparison, increased social media use may actively undermine your happiness practice. And finally, real-life social interactions are superior to digital interactions when it comes to making you happier.

---

12 Brown, "Social Media Is Broken."
13 Wirtz et al., "Social Media Subjective Well-Being," 1673.

PRACTICE HAPPINESS IN YOUR REAL LIFE

The sister of an acquaintance spends hours every day taking and posting pictures of herself on Instagram and TikTok. She is thrilled when an image receives hundreds of likes and devastated when it doesn't. Since apps like Instagram provide analytics, she gets easy access to the likability of her face every second of every day. How many people did she reach, which pictures garnered the most engagement, and which filters performed best? Because this tool allowed her to pinpoint the favorite filter among her audience, she eventually underwent plastic surgery to make her face look more like her filtered self.

Social media is like reality TV. Companies pay actors (only they're called influencers) enormous sums of money for commercials often not clearly designated as ads. We may understand rationally that most of what we see on these accounts is based on business interests, but we still respond emotionally. These businesses and platforms know how to trigger our FOMO and psychological need to keep up with the Joneses (or the Kardashians). We forget that every part is choreographed, scripted, practiced in multiple takes, then edited, photoshopped, and curated. Reality is nowhere in sight.

In Norway, social media influencers must disclose on each picture which filters they're using to make it clear to others that they are viewing an altered image. The new law aims to help reduce societal pressure of comparing oneself to heavily retouched imagery in advertising.[14] But pictures are much more powerful than text to our brains, so even if we read the disclaimer, as far as our brains are concerned, seeing is often believing.

---

14 Grant, "Influencers React to Law."

Most of the content we see on social media is purposely aspirational and often completely fake, with influencers posing in rented private jets, in front of printed vacation backgrounds, and with heavy filters akin to digital cosmetic surgery. Social media acts like a tool to separate the haves from the have-nots and as a device to pretend you belong to the haves, even when you don't. We incorrectly assume millions of people are doing great while we are not. We know that social media business models don't serve us as users, yet they are so tempting and addictive for our brains that we don't care.

We know entire teams are working on social media apps with the express purpose of hooking our brains and making us stay on their apps for as long as possible. The gamification, beautification, and sexification of apps are not for our benefit but the company's bottom line. Gamification applies game elements such as point scoring, competition, and rules as a marketing technique to drive engagement with a product or service, such as frequent flier rewards programs. Beautification creates unrealistic perfection in the appearance of images and videos via filters and retouching software, feeding our aspirational obsession with looking like Instagram models. Sexification combines sexual imagery with regular activities or products to make boring or neutral content more exciting for consumers, such as sparsely clad models using standard household products.

These tactics keep us locked in a virtual world that promises happiness but keeps it just out of reach.

The happiness practices in this book focus on our real lives rather than what we may want to project online. We need to unblur the line between reality and cyberspace and ground ourselves again in our experience of the world, relationships with family and friends, passions and interests, and meaningful contribution to our communities and the planet.

> **KEY TAKEAWAYS**
>
> - Happiness is comprised of daily positive emotions and long-term life satisfaction.
> - No matter our situation, we can start a happiness practice today.
> - Focusing on an internal happiness practice centered on what we can control is more effective than looking to external validation and circumstances to make us happy.
> - Social comparison and FOMO, especially heightened due to excessive social media use, decreases happiness and satisfaction.
> - One foundational way to start a happiness practice is to focus on the abundance rather than the lack in our lives (Exercise: Keep a Gratitude Journal for One Week).

Starting your happiness practice is about understanding the different types of happiness and satisfaction, committing to daily experiments to chart your own path, getting honest about the aspects of your life that impede your happiness, and starting with gratitude for the joy that already permeates your life.

We must identify what we have control over and can change, and accept those things outside our control. Finding the balance between these two is crucial for a happy life. Arjun taught me that there is empowerment and happiness in taking full responsibility for our attitude and response to every situation, even the challenging ones.

Unfortunately, some of us live in a self-imposed prison of our past that we must break out of before we can fully implement our happiness practice.

Chapter 2
THE PRISON OF OUR PAST

> No amount of guilt can change the past,
> and no amount of worrying can change the future.
> **—UMAR IBN AL-KHATTAAB, RELIGIOUS SCHOLAR**

My friend George killed a woman when he was sixteen.

Of course, I didn't know this when he and I met at a college coding class in Mexico in 2002. We were in our early twenties, but I could tell right away that he was more mature than our peers. He was intelligent and conscientious and a much better coder than me. As my partner for our semester project, George helped me a lot with coding, but I learned a much more important lesson from him that had nothing to do with our class.

Months into our friendship, George told me about that fateful morning when he accidentally hit a homeless woman while driving home. He couldn't brake quickly enough when she stepped into the street without warning. The woman died hours later at the hospital. George was a sixteen-year-old kid who was in the wrong place at the wrong time. He had not been texting while driving or using any substances. It was a tragic accident, but nonetheless George was charged with involuntary manslaughter several months later. The judge spared him jail time and instead ordered five years of supervision because George didn't break any laws and wasn't driving carelessly or impaired. Throughout his college years, George spent every weekend making the three-hour trek to his court-appointed supervisor, then drove straight back to school to study.

Even though he avoided jail time, George's past could have easily become a mental prison. Instead, George was grateful to the judge for giving him a second chance at life. He went to college instead of spending those prime years behind bars. Experiencing this traumatic event when he was only a teenager allowed George to see life as precious and fragile. Even though it was an accident, he took responsibility for causing the death of this woman, whose life was as valuable as his own.

Not every one of us has such a highly traumatic incident in our past, but we all have baggage. Simply saying that we have no regrets about the past doesn't honor the complexity of our experiences or the hurt we have caused others. Of course, we regret harmful behaviors and actions. However, once we become consumed with regret and worry, we are stuck in the past. We put ourselves in a prison of our own making. If our guilt and shame cause us to surrender to the past, it will define our entire lives. Accepting the fact that we can't change the past and understanding that we *can* choose how we deal with it allows us to move forward and grow from our experiences.

Even though I'm grateful George's coding skills resulted in both of us getting top marks for our semester project, I'm much more thankful for what George taught me through the way he honored the past without letting it define him. George graduated at the top of our class and became a successful consultant. He started a family, had two beautiful children, and became a respected member of his community. George used his painful past experiences to become the person he wanted to be. He also inspired me to see that his approach to honoring the past allowed him to live fully in the present and expend most of his energy where it was needed at the time—his schooling. Watching George excel and make the most of his opportunities while coping with such tragedy, inspired me to do the same. I refocused my energy on the task at hand, my education, and graduated with honors.

> **HOW DOES PROCESSING OUR PAST BENEFIT OUR HAPPINESS?**
>
> - You will own and accept your life as it is and make peace with your history.
> - You will liberate yourself from crushing guilt and resentment so you can rebuild your life.
> - You will experience gratitude and happiness alongside your pain.
> - You will feel alive again.

In this chapter, we'll discuss the different types of painful past experiences we must deal with and how to personalize our grieving process and find closure. I'll share with you the FACT framework for dealing with challenging situations from the past. We'll also dig into therapy and discuss whether or not it actually works in helping us process the past.

There are innumerable ways our past impacts our lives today, but I've found the most difficult things usually fall into one of three categories.

THE THREE CATEGORIES OF PAINFUL PAST EXPERIENCES

1. **Loss.** The most catastrophic losses can be those of loved ones, including family members and close friends. However, heartbreaking losses also include pregnancy loss, the death of beloved pets, financial catastrophes such as job losses, losing a family home to a natural disaster, and losing relationships and friendships. Additionally, we may lose our quality of life when diagnosed with a chronic or fatal illness, our freedom when incarcerated, and more abstract values like faith, identity, or self-esteem.

2. **Anger/shame/guilt/resentments.** This category deals in regret and unresolved feelings, boundaries we never set, and conversations we never had. This can include things we did that we shouldn't have done and things we didn't do that we should have done. Also in this category are the ways other people have treated us that were hurtful or unfair. Items in this category are often unspoken and might only be known to one of the parties involved.

3. **What-ifs.** We get stuck in an endless cycle of what-ifs when we let our brain run away with the paths we could have taken and the decisions we might have made but didn't. We play the what-if game if we're unhappy with our current situation or future prospects and blame our past for where we are now. We conveniently forget that there is always an opportunity

cost for each decision. Most likely, if we had made the other potential decision, we'd still play the what-if game. We all accept where we were born but relentlessly question why we don't have unlimited choice (and the ability to identify the perfect option) in every other aspect of our lives.

I find it helpful to think of the acronym FACT when processing difficult situations and feelings from my past. It's a simple way to work through a lingering issue I never quite dealt with to keep it from continually disrupting my life. Refusing to address these challenges can lead to resentment impacting my relationships, keep me stuck in the past, and prevent me from making different choices.

USE FACT TO PROCESS YOUR PAST

The FACT model includes facing and accepting our past, calibrating our response, and taking positive action.

F – ace your history with all its contradictory emotions, thoughts, beliefs, and situations. There is no way to hide from your past because you always carry it within you. Facing painful past events is difficult, but ignoring them will prevent you from moving forward.

A – ccept your past as it was. Don't ask why something happened but why it happened in a certain way. Was it something you or someone else did? Was it under your control or not? Accept the facts of the situation, even if they're hard to swallow. I remind myself repeatedly of the serenity prayer, written by American theologian Reinhold Niebuhr:

God, grant me the serenity to accept the things I cannot change, the courage to change the things I can, and the wisdom to know the difference.

C – alibrate your response. We can quickly get overwhelmed by guilt, shame, and resentment if we allow our thoughts to take control of us rather than controlling our thoughts. Focusing on facts, not beliefs and what-ifs, will help you calibrate your emotional response. I will teach you how to do this in more detail in Chapter 4.

T – ake positive action. Whether you believe everything happens for a reason, any situation can become a learning opportunity to teach valuable insights and inform future actions. Taking positive action can include self-care practices, seeking help for processing overwhelming traumatic events, and making amends with people we have wronged.

I used FACT to process the resentment I felt toward my parents for not allowing me to attend my preferred university. When it came time for me to choose a college, I'd already been away from my family for several years. I'd lived in Switzerland for the last two years of high school and graduated there. I had worked extremely hard throughout high school and was overjoyed when I was accepted into my top-choice school: Babson College in Boston, Massachusetts. It was a highly selective school and the only one that offered an entrepreneurship major at the time. It was a big deal that I even got in, and I was proud of myself. I couldn't wait to go, but when I told my parents I was accepted, they said no.

Although they supported my college aspirations in general, they didn't want four more years of our family scattered all over the place and being so far away from me that it would be hard to spend time together face-to-face. As a parent myself now, I understand their reasoning, but back then, I could only see what I wanted and that my parents weren't willing to give it to me. I couldn't afford to pay for school myself, so I had to rely on my parents' support. There was nothing I could do except hold a grudge. I eventually decided to study industrial engineering at the Technological Institute of Monterrey (ITESM) in Mexico.

I've since worked through that situation, but it left a bad taste in my mouth for years. I never discussed my resentment with my parents. However, I knew I had to process my underlying feelings, or they would continue to negatively impact our relationship.

Using FACT to work through this challenge, I first had to face the situation head-on, acknowledging that it still affected me years later. I experienced many contradictory emotions, from resentment about not getting my way to guilt for not being grateful for my parents' unwavering support for my education.

The second step was accepting the past as it was, including my embarrassment over being ungrateful toward my parents, the feeling that I had missed out on attending my first-choice college, and wondering what experiences I could have had in that alternate life. Once I accepted my complex feelings, it was much easier to accept the entire situation, including all the resulting positive events. I got an excellent education, made good friends, and had a close relationship with my family. Acceptance shifted my focus from *what could have been* to *what was*.

Having faced and accepted the situation, I could calibrate my response to focus on the facts rather than the beliefs and stories

I'd made up over years of rumination. I no longer felt intense emotions when thinking about my college days because I actively controlled my thoughts about the situation.

Finally, the last step in the FACT process is to take positive action. In this case, it wasn't an external action on my part. As I said, I never discussed the issue with my parents from the beginning. It was a matter of resolving my own complex feelings about the situation internally, and there was no need to involve anyone else. However, other cases might require an apology, honest conversation, or a change in behavior or the relationship.

Personally, I believe that everything happens for a reason and that I learned specific lessons during my university years that I could not have learned in another place or another way. I'm grateful for the life I have today, and every experience played a part in leading me to this point. I've made peace with my history. Any occasion can become a learning experience to teach you important life lessons and inform your future decisions.

If you want to try FACT, it's wise to start small. Maybe you didn't ask the girl you liked out on a date or missed out on the promotion you really wanted. Practice using FACT with a past situation that was frustrating or embarrassing but not life altering or downright devastating. Practicing how you process the past in small ways will help you once more complex and painful incidents from your past rise to the surface.

DON'T GO IT ALONE

Although I encourage you to use FACT, I know some issues and challenges will be difficult to figure out independently. Don't carry your past alone. Talk to your partner or a good friend. Go to therapy if it's accessible and affordable for you. If you're religious or spiritual, you may benefit from talking with your priest, rabbi, or meditation teacher. If your past includes addiction, traumatic injuries, or chronic illnesses, you may find solace in self-help groups and programs to deal with the most challenging aspects of your life.

I've been married to my wife for a decade, but I've only recently learned how to truly open up. During the early years of our marriage, I was unable to talk to my wife about difficult past experiences. Some of this was due to my cultural upbringing, where it was simply not acceptable for boys to cry or express negative feelings unless they were perceived as masculine emotions, such as anger. I learned to pride myself on repressing my feelings and keeping them hidden, especially when it came to sadness, shame, embarrassment, guilt, and fear.

I denied that difficult situations and events from my past still affected me emotionally or that it would help to share them with my wife. We ended up feeling disconnected from each other, and I realized that I needed to be more vulnerable about the experiences that still haunted me today.

It was uncomfortable and awkward at first because I was so conditioned to internalize my feelings. However, trusting my wife by opening up has shown me that she will have my back, no matter what. We've grown in mutual trust and openness and have gained a more nuanced understanding of each other because we know how our stories have shaped us. We've been able to help each other come to terms with hard times and struggles predating our marriage.

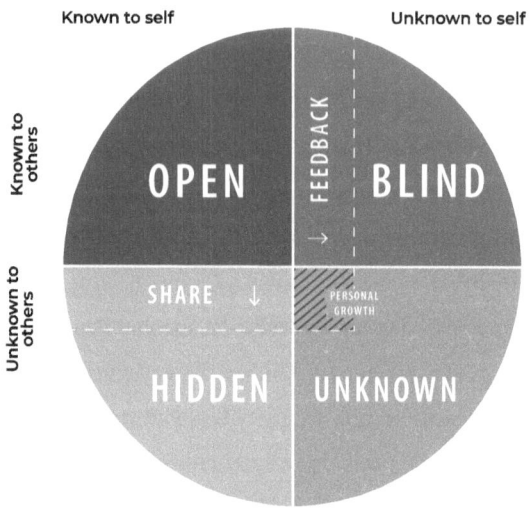

This graphic is called the Johari window, and it was created by psychologists Joseph Luft and Harrington Ingham to help people better understand themselves and their interpersonal relationships.[15] The goal is to expand the first quadrant, the open area, and shrink the other quadrants. According to Luft, it "takes energy to hide, deny, or be blind to behavior." This is precisely what I experienced in my own life. Although I thought repressing my past was a great solution, it required a lot of effort and energy to keep these experiences and resulting feelings and behaviors hidden away. When I started opening up to my wife, aspects of my past that had lived in the hidden quadrant were now transferred into the open quadrant.

Once I actively chose self-disclosure with my wife and a few close friends, my past became less overwhelming and prominent in my thoughts and emotions. Research by Mehl et al. shows that

---

15 Luft, "The Johari Window," 6.

when self-disclosure leads to more meaningful, deeper conversations, it can improve the happiness of both parties: "Deep conversations may actually make people happier. Just like self-disclosure can instill a sense of intimacy in a relationship, deep conversations may instill a sense of meaning in the interaction of partners. Therefore, our results raise the interesting possibility that happiness can be increased by facilitating substantive conversations."[16]

This openness also allowed me to learn new things about myself, which fall into the unknown quadrant. Self-reflection leads to self-awareness, which helped me better understand myself and gain clarity on who I was and what I wanted to stand for. I realized that the more I knew about myself, the easier it was to distance myself from the opinions of others, the stories I'd believed about myself for decades, and the roles I'd played since childhood. Some of our conditioning is cultural or societal, and some of it comes from parents or caregivers, peers, friends, and partners. I'm not saying this is done out of malice, but we often grow up with a label: the class clown, the goody two-shoes, the bad boy, the nerd, or the jock, for example. I'm no longer the same person I was at five, seventeen, or twenty-five years old, and I've outgrown many of the labels and roles assigned to me by others.

Knowing myself better allows me to stand up for myself and my beliefs, not in a confrontational way but calmly and firmly. I know myself and practice honestly talking about my feelings, ideas, and opinions, even if it's uncomfortable or unpopular. I'm more in tune with the spaces, situations, and people that enhance or diminish my well-being. I've decided to take off the mask, and I refuse to put it back on. I made a lot of progress on my own by

---

16 Mehl et al., "Eavesdropping on Happiness," 541.

using the FACT framework and being honest about my past, but there were other issues I knew would benefit from expert support.

Therapy is one of the primary tools that help me deal with significant past challenges.

THERAPY: DOES IT REALLY WORK?

I strongly believe in therapy and have worked with my therapist for years to address past and current challenges and how they intersect. Our past is often the key to figuring out our present behaviors and future plans. Unlocking my past has become a gold mine of understanding and personal growth. The feedback from my therapist helps me see and address the blind spot quadrant of the Johari window. I've also uncovered parts of the unknown quadrant through this increased self-examination and self-reflection.

A large 2021 meta-analysis in the journal *Nature Human Behaviour* reviewed 419 randomized controlled trials, including 53,288 research participants, to determine if specific psychological interventions increased patients' well-being.[17] The participants were a mix of individuals with diagnosed mental illnesses, physical illnesses, or neither. The last group is considered a nonclinical population—people who may access therapy for dealing with an acute difficult life situation, such as divorce, losing a child or spouse, or the addiction or illness of a loved one.

According to this analysis, the most successful therapeutic approaches are mindfulness, multicomponent positive psychology, acceptance and commitment therapy, and cognitive behavioral therapy.

---

17 Agteren et al., "Psychological Interventions to Improve Mental Wellbeing," 631.

MINDFULNESS

The meta-analysis explains that "mindfulness involves training to focus attention on one's immediate sensory situation, breath, or some visualization, and to let go of thinking about other places, the past or the future. It had small-to-moderate effects for physically ill and non-clinical populations, but had a moderate to large effect on those with mental illness."[18] The study also explains that "*reminiscence interventions*, which focus on reviewing episodes from one's past and integrating them into a more positive mindset, also had a small positive effect."[19] However, it is essential to note that the best results come from using different approaches in combination with mindfulness. For example, if you are dealing with your childhood memories of losing a family member to addiction, you may use a self-help group to process these traumatic events. Concurrently, mindfulness therapy can help to anchor you in the present moment so you don't get trapped in the past.

MULTICOMPONENT POSITIVE PSYCHOLOGY

"Positive psychology researchers focus on how people who aren't suffering from any mental disorders or deficiencies can thrive, intellectually and emotionally."[20] Often these interventions are a multipronged approach of different exercises focusing on personality and character strengths, gratitude practices, and savoring life experiences. Using this multicomponent approach provided a small effect on happiness and well-being.

---

18 Davies, "New Evidence That Therapy Can Make You Happier."
19 Davies, "New Evidence That Therapy Can Make You Happier."
20 Davies, "New Evidence That Therapy Can Make You Happier.".

ACCEPTANCE AND COMMITMENT THERAPY

These "interventions focus on building commitment to change, creating a sense of hope, and a focus on acceptance as opposed to control in one's life."[21] This sounds a lot like Niebuhr's serenity prayer, and therefore it makes sense to me that this approach works. Our past is the most obvious part of our lives we cannot change. Freedom is letting go of what we cannot control and focusing all our effort on the positive changes we can make. Acceptance and commitment therapy showed a small to moderate effect on happiness.

COGNITIVE BEHAVIORAL THERAPY

This popular method used in talk therapy attempts to improve happiness by changing dysfunctional and unhealthy thought patterns, learning emotion-regulation skills, and how to reframe life events in a more neutral or positive way. This type of therapy had a small to moderate effect when applied to people with diagnosed mental illnesses but didn't significantly affect the happiness of nonclinical populations.

This meta-analysis seems to be a vote of confidence for leveraging mindfulness to fully experience the present moment and not get stuck in the past, as one of the most efficient ways to increase our happiness. It's important to note that none of the approaches alone showed a large effect on happiness but instead a small to moderate effect. To me, these results mean that there is no silver bullet.

I believe the best way to increase happiness is to leverage complementary activities, experiment with methods, tools, and

---

21 Davies, "New Evidence That Therapy Can Make You Happier."

approaches, and create a happiness practice customized to my life and current needs. For me, this has included cognitive behavioral therapy, mindfulness training, and self-hypnosis. (We'll talk more about mindfulness and self-hypnosis in Chapter 6.)

WORKING ON THIS BOOK HAS BEEN THERAPEUTIC

Last, working on this book has allowed certain truths to float to the surface that I was no longer consciously aware of. These long-forgotten memories, although sometimes painful, will enable me to continue my journey toward integrating all the pieces of my past into my present self.

When I was in elementary school, I loved poetry and writing stories. I was intensely curious, and explaining concepts or new ideas I had learned about in front of the class or during a presentation came easy to me. Combining a love for learning with expressing my ideas verbally or in written form was second nature until the day a group of popular boys relentlessly teased and humiliated me in front of the class for expressing my opinion in a presentation. I lost all self-confidence. I shut down. I stopped talking. I became shy, quiet, and unwilling to face that kind of ridicule again.

I was simply protecting myself as best I could at the time, but my coping mechanism followed me through elementary and high school, all the way to college. Only then did I realize how much that one instance in my past had shaped my behavior for years. I finally faced the painful memory and took active steps to reteach myself confidence in front of an audience. I took a public speaking class and practiced by participating and giving presentations in my college courses. Last but not least, I'm putting myself out there with this book. Writing is shaping up to be the ultimate practice in processing the past, facing the risk of a negative response to my words, and doing it anyway.

Using FACT, opening up to loved ones, and accessing therapy have all helped me process my past.

GRIEVING THE PAST AND FINDING CLOSURE

When I was eighteen, my best friend Richard died in a tragic car crash. I was devastated and in so much pain that I felt numb. The weeks after his death were a blur, and I felt utterly alone in my grief. When I emerged from my paralysis, I still didn't know what to do with my sadness and unsuccessfully tried to get rid of it. Maybe you can relate. Sometimes the grief is so overpowering that we feel we must completely shut it out, or it will consume us whole.

Throughout my life, I've practiced setting boundaries around my grief. How long and intensely am I willing to let any situation significantly impact me? As an eighteen-year-old who'd just lost my best friend, it was my first experience with overwhelming grief, but initially, I allotted myself just three days to mourn the death of one of the most important people in my life. Of course, I soon learned that a few days weren't sufficient. Although setting these time limits has been helpful, I've learned to become more flexible in how I apply this concept to my life.

The idea of setting aside a specific time to grieve isn't a new concept. Many cultures and faith traditions have special holidays and times of mourning, such as the seven days of shiva in Judaism, a sacred time set aside for grieving the death of a loved one. The Day of the Dead in my home country of Mexico is an annual day of remembrance for family members who have passed. Memorial Day in the United States honors fallen soldiers, and All Souls Day is the Catholic Church's holy day for remembering the dead.

Setting aside a time for grief allowed me to fully surrender to my sadness and desperation without trying to ignore or minimize my feelings. Whether it's three days, three weeks, or three months, the exact amount of time set aside to grieve isn't important, as it will vary based on the specific event. Some losses will take much longer to process than others, and the most traumatic will always stay with us.

Setting a time limit is not a way to complete grief and move on as if nothing happened. However, being intentional about deciding on your own period of grief creates space and time for you to sit with the monumental change that has just transformed your life. It's a chance for your heart and mind to accept the new reality without diving straight back into your daily life. It is also a way to exert a small measure of control and choice in the wake of events that leave you feeling out of control and helpless.

You've probably heard about the five stages of grief as proposed by psychiatrist Elisabeth Kübler-Ross in her book *On Death and Dying*: denial, anger, depression, bargaining, and acceptance.[22] Kübler-Ross explains that we go through these stages chronologically to finally arrive at acceptance. Since her book was first published in 1969, however, a French study showed that many people don't experience all the stages, nor do they happen chronologically.[23] *Psychology Today* explains that the industry's idea of grief following a neat pattern has changed and that "many, if not most, people will not progress through

---

22 Kübler-Ross, *On Death and Dying*, 51–146.
23 Sauteraud, "'Stages of Grief' Do Not Exist," 93–95.

these stages."[24] Although many people eventually reach a form of acceptance of their loss, believing there is "a proper way to grieve can make the process more difficult." Instead, grief is "now understood to be highly individualized and unpredictable," so we must permit ourselves to go through the process in our own way and time frame.

Grief doesn't end or go away, but it does change and evolve over time. Finding closure doesn't mean checking grief off your list. It means not allowing grief to keep you stuck in the past but instead moving on together *with* your grief.

Whenever possible, I try to close open circles when it comes to grief. We often think of grief as losing a loved one to death. However, we can also grieve a myriad of other aspects of our life, such as the end of relationships, the loss of a belief system or quality of life. Sometimes we can go back to people we've hurt and apologize for what we have done. If we decide to do this, we must enter the process with humility and without expecting forgiveness or any specific response. We must consider if our reaching out may cause more harm than good, in which case we may choose not to interact. The same goes the other way around. Often we don't have the opportunity to make amends with people from our past due to death, distance, or the assessment that any contact or interaction would cause further hurt or damage to us. For example, if you grew up with alcoholic parents, you may have had to cut off contact to protect yourself. Finding closure does not mean you must reopen communication or restart unhealthy relationships. You can find closure within yourself.

---

24 Psychology Today, "Grief."

EXERCISE
Watch It Burn

In instances where you're seeking closure, you've probably heard the advice to write a letter and burn it. That's exactly what we're going to do here, so it's time to grab a piece of paper, a writing utensil, matches or a lighter, and a fireproof plate or receptacle.

I've done this many times, addressing letters to friends and family members from my past, expressing all my hurt and anger, and not holding anything back. I've also written a letter to my past self, listing everything I've done that made me feel ashamed or guilty. Putting down all my fears, regrets, and shortcomings without stifling myself was incredibly freeing. It is liberating to say absolutely anything in your letter, regardless of how hurtful, extreme, or untrue. Feel free to word vomit—let it all out! There is no need to censor yourself because nobody else will see this letter. I felt that proverbial weight lift off my shoulders.

It is such a simple exercise but unbelievably powerful because when you're done, you don't keep the letter or send it to the person you've addressed. Instead, you light it up and burn it. Watching your letter burn after spilling your guts is a powerful cleansing ritual. Sometimes the way to healing our relationships has nothing to do with the other person but with giving voice to our own experience and feelings, just for ourselves. For me, this letter-burning ritual often resolves resentment, anger, and disappointment, thus allowing me to move on from my past grievances. That does not mean that I will invite the person back into my life but that I no longer expend excessive amounts of energy and attention on the situation or relationship.

Whenever possible, I try to include an aspect of gratitude in my search for closure. This was especially helpful in grieving the loss of my friend Richard, long after my initial mourning period. It just goes to show that grief is processed in spurts. I developed all the rolls of film I'd accumulated during our high school years. I spent hours sorting through the pictures, reveling in all the happy, profound, and funny memories we'd made. I put them all together in a thick photo album that showcased his unique personality, the extraordinary friend he was to me, and the joy he brought to everyone fortunate enough to know him. I packed a suitcase and got on a plane to Richard's hometown. Giving Richard's mother a physical representation of what her son had meant to me was a part of my grieving process and an attempt at closure that was just as meaningful as the first few weeks of mourning in solitude.

My approach to processing this loss also included reminiscing about my experiences with Richard. I didn't know it then, but calling up these nostalgic feelings for the friendship we shared helped me process the past in a healthy way. Especially when dealing with past losses of loved ones, nostalgia can play an essential role, according to research. A 2018 study in *Psychology* found that the complex emotional state of nostalgia, or missing the past, makes us feel better, not worse. Nostalgia often combines making sense of life with social support, which promotes "emotional satisfaction and enhances subjective well-being."[25]

Finding closure takes time and many different approaches depending on the past situation you are dealing with, the people involved, and the severity of the incident. While I've shared my experiences with grieving the loss of my best friend, loss and

---

25 Rao et al., "Subjective Well-Being in Nostalgia: Effect and Mechanism," 1720.

grief take on many faces. As we discussed at the beginning of the chapter, our past may include the loss of pregnancies, beloved pets, family homes, or financial security. Grieving the past often includes both solitude and social sharing, an internal process of grief and acceptance, and an external expression of closure, whether that means burning a letter, creating a photo album, or whatever else might feel meaningful to you.

> **KEY TAKEAWAYS**
>
> ▸ Remember the FACT acronym for dealing with your past (Face it, Accept it, Calibrate your response, and Take positive action).
> ▸ Get help and resources to deal with the pain of your past—don't carry it alone.
> ▸ Excessively dwelling on the past and focusing on what we've lost can blind us to new opportunities right now.
> ▸ You are not defined by the worst thing that's ever happened to you or that you've ever done to someone else.
> ▸ You can move forward *with* your past, rather than moving on *from* your past.

We can't change our past, but we can accept it and move forward. If we don't acknowledge our history, it will keep us from living in the present and making plans for the future. The weight of the past will drag us down, leaving us unable to rise above the worst thing that happened to us or that we inflicted on others.

Instead of *getting over* the loss of a loved one, you must learn to live with it. You get to choose how to mourn. Moving forward is different from moving on. It doesn't mean forgetting about what happened. It means accepting that life brings both horror and joy, and you can press forward, holding both in your heart. German poet Rainer Maria Rilke reminds us, "Let everything happen to you, beauty and terror, just keep going, no feeling is final."

You will not move on from the worst tragedies that have ever happened to you. As my wife, Cynthia, says, you will heal and you will rebuild yourself around the loss you have suffered. You decide whether this event will define you. You will never be the same, nor would you want to be, but you will be whole again.

Making peace with your story and fully owning the one precious life you have can induce a powerful shift in your perspective.

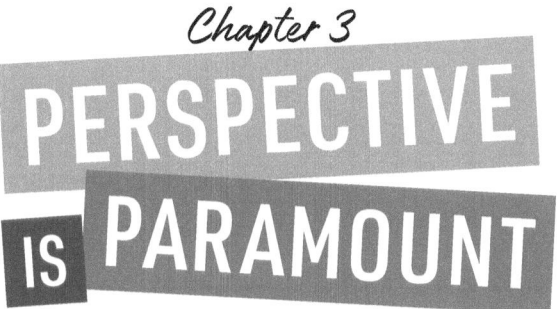

Chapter 3
PERSPECTIVE IS PARAMOUNT

> We see the world, not as it is, but as we are—
> or, as we are conditioned to see it.
> **—STEPHEN R. COVEY, AUTHOR**

A loud crack startled me upright in my seat. I didn't know then it was a malfunctioning turbine. My stomach turned as the plane sharply tilted and dropped before righting itself. The feeling of that first moment on a roller coaster plunging from the highest point, when your breath catches in your throat and your guts slam against your rib cage, is fun at an amusement park. It felt a lot less fun as a little boy on a plane for the first time. Sitting next to me was my grandmother, who quietly started praying. I was terrified. What is etched in my mind as a horrifying near-death experience was likely just above-average turbulence, and never a real threat to my life, but it didn't feel like that in the moment.

As a kid on my first plane ride, I had no perspective on whether I was in real danger because I had no other experiences for the purposes of comparison. Even adults who are experienced fliers often perceive plane travel as riskier than driving their car to work every day, despite the fact that statistics confirm plane travel is the safer transportation option. We tend to feel safer in situations we can exert control of (or at least situations in which we perceive the illusion of control). Our perspective on the relative safety of being in a car versus a plane—or anything else, for that matter—has little to do with the actual risk and everything with the stories we tell ourselves.

As an adult, I got my pilot's license and learned everything I could about aviation. I decided to actively change my perspective on airplane travel, which had been skewed by my scary experience as a child. And maybe part of it was also reclaiming some control that I felt I lost when sitting in my seat, buckled in, unable to do anything but hope and hold on to my grandmother. In the pilot seat, I at least regained the idea of control. But more than that, educating myself helped me reframe my thinking. Turbulence is just like a bumpy road but in the air! Taking this perspective made all the difference. I travel a lot for work and to see family, so I've experienced plenty of turbulence since that first time, some as bad or worse, but I've never felt the same terror because my perspective has changed.

In this chapter, we'll discuss why our brains are hardwired to adopt certain perspectives over others and how we can retrain our minds. We'll talk about the different cognitive distortions that impact our decision making and do an exercise together that will leave you questioning your eyesight.

But first, why should you care about challenging your perspectives in your happiness practice?

PERSPECTIVE AND HAPPINESS

Several studies have reported a strange finding: bronze medalists are consistently happier than silver medalists.[26] On the face, it makes no sense because the silver medalists did better and therefore should be happier, right? Well, it appears that perspective makes all the difference. Even though the silver medalists feel disappointed about missing out on the gold, bronze medalists tend to focus on the fact that they made it onto the podium at all.

Our perspective about a specific event or the world as a whole impacts our outlook on life. How we define, frame, and interpret situations affects our emotional state. It's a bit of a chicken versus egg situation, as the research isn't entirely clear on whether less happy people are prone to take a more negative perspective, or if framing a situation negatively makes people less happy. Possibly, both are true.

Writer Seph Fontane Pennock cites happiness researcher Sonja Lyubomirsky who found that "happy individuals perceive, interpret, and subsequently think about life events and life circumstances in more positive ways than negative ones. These differences in cognitive processes may, in turn, reinforce and promote people's affective dispositions."[27] Pennock continues to say that an "individual's definition of an event (threat or challenge), his or her interpretations, and the ways in which he or she continues to think about the event (e.g., with a sense of tragedy, a sense of humor, ruminating about the past) can have a big impact on his or her outlook." In other words, more than the facts of the situation, it's how we view those facts in the context of our beliefs, circumstances, and personality that matters.

---

26 Hedgcock, Luangrath, and Webster, "Thinking and Expressions among Olympic Medalists," e13-e21.
27 Fontane Pennock, "Hedonic Treadmill."

As with specific situations like my childhood fear of flying, our perspective on the world, in general, is also heavily informed by our experiences rather than facts. Our unique worldview directly relates to our thoughts and feelings, however distorted and incorrect they might sometimes be. As humans, we look for patterns. We try to make sense of an often chaotic and complicated world. We don't like uncertainty and unpredictability, so we're more comfortable creating a narrative in our heads that makes the world make sense, even if that narrative is wrong. In other words, humans are more comfortable with *any story* than *no story*.

Coming up with a narrative provides us with a sense of security, but it also skews our perspective. This sense making helps keep our brains from becoming overwhelmed by the extreme uncertainty of life. Still, as Immanuel Kant admonished us, we must remember that our worldview is merely a projection, not the thing itself. There is no way to stop our brains from doing this altogether, but we are not forced to react to this hard wiring. Author Stephen R. Covey famously advises us that we have a choice to change the story. We can adapt our perspective and decide on our response. As he puts it, "Between stimulus and response there is a space. In that space is our power to choose our response. In our response lies our growth and our freedom."[28]

Understanding that we view the world through our own personal lens can be freeing. This knowledge can create the distance necessary to look at something from a different angle, find an unlikely solution, or see a situation, person, or relationship in a new light. Having a measure of control, freedom, and autonomy improves our outlook and emotional state.

---

28 Covey, Foreword to *Lead or Get Off the Pot!*, xiv.

WHAT ARE THE BENEFITS OF CHALLENGING OUR PERSPECTIVES?

- You will understand your perspective through the lens of your unique life experiences.
- You will be able to reframe challenging situations.
- You will create more empathy and understanding in your relationships.
- You will understand how rigid perspectives can cloud your judgment and how to dismantle them to make better decisions.

We often forget that this relates not only to material aspects of our life but to our mental landscape as well. In his book, *Man's Search for Meaning*, Austrian psychiatrist and Holocaust survivor Viktor Frankl explains, "Everything can be taken from a man but one thing: the last of the human freedoms—to choose one's attitude in any given set of circumstances, to choose one's own way." Although many of us will never be in a situation as grave as a concentration camp in the Holocaust, Frankl's realization that autonomy and freedom extend to our inner worlds, even in circumstances that rob us of most external choices, applies to all of us. Especially in situations where we do not control the events or outcomes, even if it's *only* being stuck on a plane during turbulence, we have the power and freedom to control our perspective and response.

According to Howell in the *Journal of Happiness Studies*, self-determination or autonomy is an indicator of increased happiness because "psychological well-being correlates positively with psychological need for satisfaction," including the need for autonomy.[29]

---

29 Howell et al., "Momentary Happiness," 1.

I believe this extends to the most extreme situations, such as Frankl's, where all we can do is change our insides because we have zero control over the outside. This is not to say that we could or should experience profound happiness and joy in the most devastating and cruel situations or that we are to blame if we fail to do so. However, reflecting on our thought patterns and stories and changing our perspective can soften our suffering, create a small space for momentary relief, and allow tiny moments of contentment and levity, even during our darkest times.

Aside from our lives' most difficult moments, perspective affects our emotional state in everyday contexts and mundane situations. As with so many things, the first step is awareness of the most common biases we tend to hold. These biases skew our perspective to the point of negatively impacting our emotional state, impairing our judgment, and making bad decisions. Renowned psychologists Daniel Kahneman and Amos Tversky first described these thinking errors in the 1970s. This framework has stood the test of time. We'll talk through some of the most common cognitive distortions and biases that impact our perspective and decision making, as well as how to start identifying and reframing them.

One of the primary reasons this is important for our happiness practice is that we often try to pinpoint which decisions in our lives have caused us to be happy or miserable. Still, we rarely think about how we made those decisions in the first place. If our choices were based on distorted thoughts, biases, and skewed perspectives, the decision might not produce the desired outcome. Of course, no decision is guaranteed to make us happy, but decisions based on erroneous attitudes are much more likely to make us miserable.

Let's dive into Kahneman and Tversky's concepts and get to know the inner workings of our brains.

COGNITIVE DISTORTIONS AND BIASES

One of the most well-known cognitive biases Kahneman and Tversky popularized is *confirmation bias*. That is, we seek out information that confirms our ideas and opinions rather than purposely looking for information that challenges our preconceptions.

We tend to be very invested in our own perspectives. We like to find information that allows us to hold on to ideas rather than doing the more complex work of questioning and possibly changing them and our behavior. We try to avoid this *cognitive dissonance* between our beliefs and contradicting evidence. Confirmation bias does make us happier temporarily, but it doesn't make us smarter. It causes less friction in our minds than the cognitive dissonance that comes with challenging our ideas. But it also keeps us from sound decision making, which significantly impacts our happiness. Think of it this way: you can either make your brain more comfortable in the moment or deal with the discomfort now for a better outcome later.

Friedrich Nietzsche said, "Convictions are more dangerous enemies of truth than lies," which I take to mean that once we have an incentive to believe something incorrect, it is more difficult to dismantle than a simple lie we are not emotionally loyal to. This *belief persistence* is another type of bias that makes our minds more likely to hold on to the stories we tell ourselves rather than accepting the facts.

EVERYONE IS LOOKING AT YOU—OR *ARE* THEY?

The *spotlight* effect is our tendency to focus on ourselves. This results in worrying that others will scrutinize everything we do and say and notice minute details about our appearance and behavior. We are constantly aware of our flaws, mistakes, and errors and believe everyone around us is as well. Most people feel that way, which means we're all walking around thinking people will notice the tiny zit on our chin, the awkward pause in our presentation, or the toothpaste stain on our shirt. But do you notice all these small details about other people you talk to in the checkout line or at a work meeting? Probably not. And even if you happened to see one of those details, you certainly didn't notice the thirty-eight other items on their list.

This leads to an ironic dynamic: many of us are worried about facing scrutiny from others, while those others aren't paying any attention to our flaws because they're concerned about facing scrutiny from us. This can prevent us from trying out a new hobby, advocating for ourselves in a work meeting, or deciding against wearing that brightly colored shirt. We're worried about other people's judgment and scrutiny, even if doing these things would add to our momentary happiness or life satisfaction.

Although this human tendency of being a bit self-centered can result in feelings of insecurity and awkwardness, at the other end of the spectrum, it may also result in being overconfident in our performance. Even though, statistically, most of us fall in the middle of the bell curve (in other words, we're average), we tend to believe that we're better than most. If we performed in a singing competition exactly the same as a stranger did, it would be easier for us to correctly judge their performance than our own because we're biased in our own favor. Not having a realistic idea of our skills and performance can lead to a rude awakening in situations where we're judged on the facts or by external factors or individuals, such as an employee review or an official contest with judges.

We also tend to think that we are faster and more efficient than others, leading to the *planning fallacy*. In other words, we underestimate how much time and energy a task will take us because we think we're more capable than others, so we allot less time than we think the average person may take on a project. It's necessary to understand that we're not exceptional when it comes to getting things done.

Whether we're engineers, wedding planners, or students writing homework essays, we should estimate the time it will take us based on what we think it would take someone else. This trick can allow us to be more accurate than if we think only about ourselves.

How does this make us happier? Adjusting our perspective changes our expectations of ourselves to be more realistic, which reduces the likelihood of failure and the accompanying negative emotions.

ANECDOTAL EVIDENCE SKEWS OUR PERSPECTIVE

The *law of small numbers* explains how we use our own experiences as a measuring stick for life in general. We believe in our own experiences more than statistics and research because we value personal interaction over indirect learning. For example, if we have one bad experience with a physician, we might extrapolate that into an opinion about the medical profession as a whole. This can lead to mistakenly painting groups of people, populations, ideas, and cultures in an overly positive or negative light based on what is actually an isolated experience. In other words, we take a tiny sample and exaggerate the degree to which it represents the entire population. This may make us happier or more optimistic if we've had overwhelmingly positive experiences, but it's only a matter of time until a negative experience changes our minds.

Overall, it will make us happier and more content to contextualize our personal experiences within more comprehensive statistics. We'll understand that sometimes we're one of the few lucky or unlucky ones instead of viewing our potentially rare experience as a common occurrence.

HOT HANDS AND PERFECT STREAKS

Have you ever gambled in Vegas and caught yourself thinking, "Red is coming up next!" after hitting black five times in a row? Our brains balk at the idea that gambling is truly unpredictable and random. So we keep putting our hard-earned money into slot machines and buy more chips, even though *cold* machines are not due for a jackpot, and black isn't due after red at the roulette table. This is an example of the *gambler's fallacy*, which is the mistaken belief that random statistical trials balance out.

Think of a time you've watched professional baseball or free throws during a basketball game. Have you ever turned to the person sitting on the couch next to you between bites of hot wings, exclaiming that a player is "on fire" or on a "streak"? The *hot-hand* fallacy explains why we think a person is doing exceptionally well or consistently horrible. We believe it's some magical streak they're riding or breaking, rather than a combination of preparation, practice, environment, and daily form resulting in an outcome we can't predict.

Because humans have evolved to identify and understand patterns, it's very tempting to seek them even in places where they can't be found, such as casinos. Accepting true randomness is difficult for humans, so understanding that our brains are prone to believe the gambler's and hot-hand fallacies doesn't inherently make us happier. However, reminding ourselves of their existence may allow us to make better decisions instead of gambling away our rent money, which will most definitely decrease our happiness.

We often use our own experiences to gauge the general probability of an event, which is called the *availability heuristic*. For example, if you had a heart attack six months ago and I asked you today how likely it is that people of your age and health become victims of heart attacks, you would probably guess higher than if I'd asked you seven months ago, before your own heart attack. Once something has happened to us or someone we know, we believe this incident is much more likely to occur. In other words, examples of occurrences are more available in our minds and memories now than before, so the event seems more probable.

It works the other way around, too. Teenage kids with brand-new driver's licenses don't think they'll get into a car accident driving to school tomorrow, even though teens between sixteen and nineteen are more likely to have fatal motor vehicle accidents than any other age group.[30] We tend to consider faulty probabilistic thinking as fact and truth because we weigh our own experiences and ideas more heavily than evidence and statistics. We're often wrong about where the actual dangers lie and what is most and least likely to happen to our kids or us.

An increase in anxiety and worry about future events that are unlikely to happen can still have the power to rob us of happiness and satisfaction in the moment.

---

30 US Centers for Disease Control and Prevention, "Teen Drivers."

JUDGING A BOOK BY ITS COVER

Consider this helpful illustration from The Decision Lab: "Let's say you're going to a concert with your friend, Sarah. Sarah has also invited two of her friends, whom you've never met before. You know that one of them is a mathematician, while the other one is a musician. When you finally meet Sarah's friends, John and Adam, you see that John wears glasses and is a bit shy, while Adam is more outgoing and dressed in a T-shirt and jeans. Without asking what they do for a living, you assume that John must be the mathematician and Adam must be the musician. You later find out that you were mistaken: Adam does math, and John plays music."[31]

We often ascribe stereotypes to people, roles, or positions merely because of those labels rather than objective evidence. This is also called the *representativeness heuristic*. We make an incorrect judgment based on ascribing certain characteristics to a specific person because they represent a group of people stereotypically associated with those characteristics. The people we surround ourselves with play a significant role in our happiness, especially if our relationships and conversations go beyond the superficial (more on this in Chapter 6). Honest, profound interactions with people we care about and whose company we genuinely appreciate can only develop if we let go of stereotypes and get to know each person as an individual.

REWRITING THE PAST

Whether something does or doesn't happen, *hindsight bias* is why we exclaim, "I told you so!" or "I knew it all along!" when we absolutely didn't. We only understand life backward, but we pretend

[31] The Decision Lab, "Similarity to Gauge Probability."

that's not the case. Once something does happen, it's almost impossible for our brains to act like we didn't know. We deny how wrong our predictions usually are and tell ourselves that whatever happened was inevitable.

This is also related to the *curse of knowledge* because our brains balk at going back to before we knew whatever it is we learned. Once we know something new, it's easy to become a little arrogant toward people who are still ignorant of one fact or another. It's important to remember that our perspectives can change instantly with new information and to be patient with others who haven't received the same information simultaneously. I certainly hope others will treat me with the same patience if I'm the ignorant one.

Another way our perspective on a situation can be skewed is *anchoring*. You may have heard of this tactic in the context of negotiations for salaries. Throwing out an extremely low-ball offer might offend a job candidate, but it can also act as an anchor that pulls the entire conversation in a specific direction. As a result, the candidate may ultimately settle for a salary significantly higher than the original offer but lower than the market rate. This happens because our brains can't help but compare the outcome to the original anchor and so we base our perspective on the comparison rather than the actual numbers. We may walk away from a salary negotiation unhappy but unable to pinpoint why.

One way to avoid falling prey to anchoring is to compare the actual outcome of a situation to the one you deemed reasonable going in, rather than the extremely high or low anchor the other party introduced. That may help prevent you from agreeing to terms based on the other person's previous anchoring maneuver rather than the facts of the situation.

Although skewed perspectives can make us more or less happy

in the moment, the bigger issue is that they significantly impact our decision making, dramatically affecting our happiness and satisfaction in the long term.

PERSPECTIVE AND DECISION MAKING

Kahneman and Tversky's *prospect theory* helps us understand how we judge the risk of any given situation and make decisions. The theory breaks the decision-making process into three aspects: framing, weighting, and valuing.

FRAMING

Say you are a government health employee framing a policy decision to deal with the COVID-19 pandemic. You might prepare a vaccine recommendation in terms of how many lives can be saved if it is followed, or how many lives may be lost if it isn't. Which approach will make it more likely that people will follow the recommendation? If you answered the latter, you're correct because humans are loss averse. In other words, losses hurt us much more than gains make us feel good. Losing a $100 bill makes us feel worse than finding the same bill makes us feel good. Thinking of how many people might die triggers a more significant emotional response than saving the same number of people.

Even if the outcome is the same both ways, a loss frame will always activate our brains more. To be as neutral as possible in our decision making, we may want to reframe a problem from a loss statement to a gain statement and vice versa. This helps our brains consider the facts of the situation instead of defaulting to an emotional response that may lead us to commit to a decision that does not increase our long-term happiness.

WEIGHTING

Remember the example about teen drivers underestimating their risks for serious car accidents? This speaks to our general problem with weighing risks appropriately, and it's true across the board. We underestimate the probability of events that are statistically much more common than we believe. On the flip side, we overestimate the likelihood of rare occurrences, like winning the lottery. Outcomes that don't match our positive expectations often result in disappointment. Conversely, worrying about negative outcomes that are very unlikely to happen can cause emotional stress and anxiety. Keeping a rational, realistic perspective of risks takes active consideration and necessitates that we retrain our brain, but it's worth it.

VALUE

Value goes back to our loss aversion. When making decisions, we try to figure out a reference point and how likely it is that the outcome will fall below (loss) or above (gain).

You would think that because losses hurt more than gains, we would be less likely to make decisions that result in losses. As long as we're in the gain domain, we behave risk averse. However, there is a little quirk in the system once we're in the loss domain called the *disposition effect*.

Nick Leeson, a derivatives trader at Barings Bank, the UK's oldest merchant bank, had been very successful for quite some time before starting to incur bigger and bigger losses. Instead of stopping the bleeding, he took on riskier trades to make back the money he'd already lost. Leeson ended up bankrupting Barings Bank and spending years in prison.[32]

---

32 Smith, "The Barings Collapse."

The more we perceive ourselves to be in the loss domain, the higher risks we are willing to take, believing our Hail Mary passes will turn it all around at the last second. Leeson's example is extreme, but it illustrates what can happen when we fall victim to our brain's natural tendencies. Of course, other factors are at play here, such as DNA, personality, and circumstances. However, it's important to remember that aligning our perspective with reality so we can make sound decisions can keep us from taking the wrong turns in everyday life and avoid the occasional life-altering choice.

EXERCISE
Duck or Rabbit? Challenge Your Perspective

Look at the graphic. What do you see when you look at the picture?

Some of us see a duck, and some of us see a rabbit. Neither one of us is wrong.

Now that you've read that, you're probably looking to find both the duck and the rabbit, which perfectly illustrates what we're trying to accomplish in rewiring our brains to be less susceptible to skewed perspectives. It takes an active effort to challenge ourselves, see situations from all angles, and understand different perspectives others may bring to a conversation.

It's a great illustration of the fact that we all have a natural tendency to think our perspective is correct, even if others are just as valid. Our perspective is merely that, a perspective—one out of multiple, often equally reasonable options. We are biased to think that our perspective is superior to others, which bleeds into our judgment of situations and people. Optical illusions are a good reminder that our brains constantly want to persuade us that we see things as they are because it removes uncertainty.

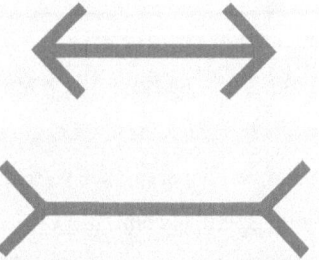

The Müller-Lyer illusion above shows two lines with arrows. If you're like most people, you will perceive that the bottom line is longer than the top line. If you take out a ruler and measure, you will find that both lines are the same length.

Our judgment and decision making are prone to the same kind of biases as our perceptual system. Watching the duck merge into the rabbit and back again can feel disorienting because our brains are uncomfortable with this duality of two conflicting perspectives.

Most important topics and life decisions don't have clear-cut black-and-white answers, but honing your skills of challenging your perspective will lessen your discomfort with holding two opposing viewpoints in your head simultaneously. The more you practice considering different perspectives, the more nuanced your reasoning and decision making will become.

YOU ARE HUMAN

Show me a perfectly rational person, and I'll show you a unicorn! Don't beat yourself up about your tendency toward certain cognitive biases and erroneous thought patterns. We all have them. They're part of being human. Our brains have evolved to survive by finding patterns, generalizing our experiences, and being highly loss averse. The less time and effort we spend berating ourselves or denying our thinking errors, the more energy we free up for making positive changes that impact our happiness.

I attended a management course at INSEAD taught by Professor Neil Bearden, who explained that the point isn't to eliminate biases from our thinking. Which is good because it's impossible to do so. There is no simple, five-step hack to free oneself of biases. That energy is better spent becoming aware of our biases and being very intentional and cautious when making a judgment or weighing a decision. The more curious we are when identifying our own biases, the more practice we'll get naming and analyzing them. This work helps us slowly rewire our brains to avoid the most common pitfalls.

USING PERSPECTIVE TO REFRAME BAD OUTCOMES

I lived in Singapore for a few months as part of my MBA. While I was there, a new Italian restaurant was opening in a beautiful plaza. There was a lot of talk about it. The cook was supposed to be great, the restaurant gorgeous, and the location perfect. But two weeks before the grand opening, a durian store opened right next door to the restaurant. The restaurant closed a month after opening.

Durian is an infamous fruit native to Singapore that has a custard-like texture and is extremely popular and quite healthy.

Sounds good, right? Well, unfortunately, the smell of durian has been described as that of raw sewage or rotting flesh mixed with onions and wet gym socks. In fact, its stench is so unbearable that durian is forbidden on public transportation. Even though the Italian restaurant owners did their due diligence and invested a lot of time, money, and effort to ensure everything was just right for their new place, they had no control over the store moving in next door. They controlled everything they could, but in the end, one humble, stinky fruit killed their project.

Too often, we choose one extreme perspective. An old proverb says every rope has two ends, but it's easier to just focus on the end you're holding. In other words, we want to believe we're in control, whether we experience success or failure. This makes us feel like we could do something differently next time to get a different outcome. But the truth is that even if you do everything right, random, unpredictable, and uncontrollable events happen and interfere with your plans. It's not your fault. The uncertainty of life is like air. It surrounds us, but we are blind to it.

We must change our perspective to allow for the fact that even if we are mindful of our thoughts, weigh decisions carefully, do our due diligence, and proceed rationally, we may achieve a below-average or even catastrophic outcome. Holding on to the illusion of control, instead of adopting the perspective that we do not have power over the entire world around us, can make us profoundly unhappy. We add insult to injury by criticizing ourselves for not seeing it coming, or ruminating over our decisions when our best option might be to accept our losses and move on.

> **KEY TAKEAWAYS**
>
> - What we consider truth is often our unique perspective skewed by cognitive distortions that have no sound empirical basis.
> - Test your beliefs and ideas even if it makes you uncomfortable.
> - Analyze the unique lens through which you perceive the world to make better decisions.
> - Once we can clearly see how we frame the world, we can dismantle our biases and change the narrative of our lives (Exercise: Duck or Rabbit? Challenge Your Perspective).

To enjoy a happy life, it is crucial to understand that our perspectives are rarely the truth. Once we recognize this, we are able to make the conscious decision to accept new information. This will allow us to come ever closer to something approximating truth and reality. Liberating ourselves from the stories we've told ourselves for years or decades and dismantling our thinking errors can lead to better decision making, which in turn positively impacts our satisfaction and happiness—not just in the moment but throughout our lives.

Our biases and distorted perspectives have profoundly impacted every aspect of our lives. Think of what we can do once we harness the power of ideas for our own good!

Chapter 4
THE POWER OF IDEAS

> As you think, so shall you become.
> **—BRUCE LEE, ACTOR**

When I was thirty-two, my mentor and business partner Joe died in a helicopter crash. He was a secondary father figure, a man I loved and admired greatly. The accident was especially tragic because Joe's son was also on the helicopter and died with him. My heart hurt for my own loss and for Joe's family. The shocking news reached me while I was on vacation in London. I felt like a deer in the headlights, immobile and stunned. As I jumped on the first available flight to Mexico, my brain was on overdrive with all the conflicting thoughts and emotions rushing through me at lightning speed. Aside from losing my close friend and mentor, I was now also left on my own to navigate our business.

My decisions would impact so many other people's livelihoods, and I could no longer discuss these concerns with the man who'd been my trusted advisor. I obsessed over the potential implications for the business. I magnified every catastrophic scenario in my head, gave in to negative assumptions about our partners and investors, and discounted my ability to confront the situation. It took days to disentangle myself from all these cognitive distortions brought on by the intense shock and grief. Even at that, it was still an incredibly difficult situation to manage, but this slightly clearer view of reality allowed me to charge ahead to meet the company's challenges.

I focused on the present and the tasks in front of me. I made a list of issues ranked by priority and divided them into smaller steps. I earned tiny wins as I started completing the steps, which kept me going for another day and another challenge. I tried to listen only to advice that was thoughtful and measured, rather than emotionally compromised. Tempers flared during that time, and emotions were a constant roller coaster for everyone involved. I could not allow myself to be sucked into the vortex of despair, or else the company would crumble and we all would be out of our jobs and livelihoods.

THE DYNAMICS BETWEEN OUR THOUGHTS AND FEELINGS

Losing Joe was an intensely emotional experience, while taking over the business required thoughtfulness and strategy. I was thrown into the deep end of the pool, desperately trying to figure out how to keep a calm head and navigate the company through years of uncertainty, while honoring the profound loss I had experienced.

It didn't occur to me until much later that I buried my feelings to focus on logistics instead. I didn't give myself the chance to properly grieve this very personal loss. Instead, I dived into four years of business restructuring and succession litigation. This was necessary, of course, but it came at the expense of suppressing my emotions. When I praise the power of ideas, I don't advise you to stuff your feelings and think happy thoughts. Emotional repression can cause severe health problems, and eventually, you will have to face your intense sadness, as I did.

Instead, I'm suggesting that we need to use our minds and thoughts to identify, label, and process our emotions instead of burying our feelings or being swallowed whole by them. Our thoughts can be a supporting framework to deal with emotions, not a way to pretend they don't exist or aren't important. These kinds of highly complex and emotionally painful situations are challenging to navigate. It's difficult to prevent ourselves from falling into distorted thinking, repressing our emotions, and focusing only on one narrow aspect of the whole because our brains are so overwhelmed.

Dealing with Joe's death showed me that I needed to make significant changes in how I lived my life, both personally and professionally. It would take almost five years for me to sort out the business concerns and allow myself to finally grieve by starting therapy and opening up to family and colleagues. A friend in my Young Presidents Organization (YPO) chapter challenged me to confront my lingering grief and sadness. I realized I had never fully dealt with the gravity of my personal loss.

This experience convinced me that one crucial way of creating more happiness in my life is to practice harnessing the power of my thoughts before tough situations arise. I was blindsided when Joe died, and I had no resources or practices in place to keep my mind from spiraling. I know more challenges will come my way, but I will not be as ill-prepared as I was back then.

> ## WHAT ARE THE BENEFITS OF HARNESSING THE POWER OF YOUR THOUGHTS?
>
> - You will learn how to use your mind to influence your emotional state and happiness.
> - You will be able to feel and process your emotions without being consumed by them.
> - You will learn how to spot cognitive distortions in yourself and others.

Accidents, illnesses, natural disasters, and even bad timing can alter our lives in a split second. The thoughts and ideas we allow our minds to dwell on can either accelerate or sabotage our progress, especially during those most difficult seasons of life. We don't control these events that have the power to significantly impact our lives and happiness, but we do control how we respond, as Viktor Frankl told us in the previous chapter.

Our mind is our most incredible tool. As with any tool, we can use it to build, create, and advance us to greatness or let it hinder and trap us. In this chapter, we'll talk about how ideas and thoughts influence our emotions and feelings. We'll discuss common thought distortions and their impact on our happiness. We'll examine how our ideas about our kids influence our parenting and do a practical exercise for reframing our thoughts.

For a long time, I was confused about how my thoughts and emotions interacted and influenced each other. But then I learned from a professor who finally helped me make sense of it.

EMOTIONS ARE LIKE DUCKLINGS

When I was studying for my MBA in Singapore, I took a class called Psychological Issues in Management. Professor Allan Filipowicz completely changed my perspective on the connection between emotions and ideas. I believed that depending on my mood or emotional state of mind, certain ideas and concepts would come to mind. For example, if I felt blue, cue sad thoughts. If I felt happy, the hopeful and bright ideas weren't far behind.

Professor Filipowicz turned this notion inside out and upside down. He explained that emotions follow an idea like ducklings follow their mother duck. Although we can't control the feelings or emotions that arise in us, we *can* control our thoughts and ideas. In essence, my professor taught me that I could populate my mind with specific ideas, and the fitting emotions would follow. If I purposely chose a positive mindset, it would be as if my brain told my body to produce the requisite positive emotions to accompany my thoughts.

I'm not advocating for toxic positivity, which is a dysfunctional approach to emotional management where people do not fully acknowledge negative emotions, particularly anger and sadness, and "involves dismissing negative emotions and responding to distress with false reassurances rather than empathy."[33] What I'm suggesting is that for me, it was a revelation that my thoughts caused my emotions and not the other way around, so I started investigating my feelings in a different way.

Learning that thoughts drive emotions helped me look at life differently. Do you remember when the stock market fell 35 percent in March 2020? Just reading this, you might feel a slight echo

---

33 Princing, "Toxic Positivity."

of your thoughts and emotions that day. Maybe you thought, *I'm going to lose my job*. Perhaps the first thing that came to mind was, *I'm going to get evicted*, or *I just lost thousands in retirement savings*. I'm willing to bet that these thoughts almost immediately led to feeling scared, anxious, or angry. Unfortunately, we are prone to make decisions from that place of emotional distress. Based on the specific combination of emotions we're feeling, our risk tolerance or loss avoidance might increase or decrease. What's missing in this process that seems almost automatic or inevitable is one critical step—asking yourself, *Do my thoughts and emotions accurately reflect what's happening?*

Again, the objective is not to wave away difficult emotions but to ask what came before them. What are you afraid of? What stories are you telling yourself? What cognitive distortions have crept in? Are your thoughts realistic and measured or hyperbolic and fatalistic?

Once we consider the validity of these thoughts, we can reframe them if necessary, which causes a recalibration or adjustment of the resulting feelings. Even in cases where our emotions are congruent with reality, this concept can help. If you lose a loved one, for example, you will experience intense grief and sadness. Your initial thoughts causing the emotions, such as that you will not see them again in this life, are correct and should not be dismissed. But you may also find other thoughts swirling around in your head that are not true such as, *I will never be happy again* or *I will be alone for the rest of my life*. Identifying these incorrect thoughts and replacing them with more reasonable ones can help such as, *I will always miss them, but I will also smile and laugh again*.

You can actively trigger thoughts of appreciation for the time you spent together, the lessons you learned from the person, or recollect times they made you laugh and feel loved. These thoughts will likely spur corresponding emotions of warmth, love, and gratitude. They don't minimize your feelings of grief but rather add a dimension of complexity.

Although we tend to look to examples on the extremes of the spectrum, it's important to remember how everyday thoughts about mundane occurrences are critical to our emotional landscape. How much power over our lives and happiness are we abdicating by considering our thoughts and feelings facts?

YOU ARE NOT YOUR FEELINGS

Environmental conditions affect us depending on the intensity of the experience, our past coping behaviors, and our personality. A rainy day will affect us less than having a dramatic fight with our best friend. Unless, maybe, we suffer from seasonal affective disorder (SAD), and it's now May and still gloomy. Generally, if the intensity of the trigger is high enough—a point that's different for every person—a fight-or-flight response ensues. We can feel the increased heart rate, blood pressure, and blood flow to major muscle groups, resulting in breathing harder, sweating, or shaking. We experience such bodily sensations as anger, anxiety, fear, frustration, or hopelessness. The repeated triggering of these responses leads to an increased susceptibility that similar triggers will result in more extreme reactions in the future.

It takes more effort to repress emotions than to feel and name them. Suppression uses up finite regulatory resources. Depleting these self-regulatory resources hurts us in other aspects because it decreases our discipline, willpower, critical thinking, and decision-making capabilities. Suppressing my feelings led to trouble sleeping, anger, rashness and impulsivity, and shutting myself off from others.

Even today, people still tend to repress socially unacceptable emotions associated with their gender. Psychologist Tabitha Kirkland "notes that emotion is gendered: Boys aren't encouraged to express emotions except those that reflect power, such as anger, whereas girls are encouraged to express their emotions but only ones that are seen as less powerful, such as agreeableness. These gendered differences in emotion socialization can lead men to suppress their emotions and can lead women to feel pressured to show positive feelings that may be inauthentic."[34]

We must counteract this emotional repression for our psychological health and well-being. A 2017 study showed accepting negative emotions and thoughts brought psychological health benefits. The researchers proposed that this increase in well-being may be "due to the role acceptance plays in negative emotional responses to stressors: acceptance helps keep individuals from reacting to—and thus exacerbating—their negative mental experiences…Overall, these results suggest that individuals who accept rather than judge their mental experiences may attain better psychological health, in part because acceptance helps them experience less negative emotion in response to stressors."[35]

FEELINGS ARE CONTAGIOUS

Have you heard the expression *emotional contagion*? This concept, popularized by cognitive psychologist Arthur S. Reber, explains how our emotions spread to the people around us as if they were

---

34 Princing, "Toxic Positivity."
35 Ford et al., "Psychological Benefits of Accepting Negative Emotions and Thoughts," 1075.

contagious.[36] Our family and friends can catch feelings—ours! Of course, the same applies to how we respond to being in the presence of people with strong emotions. It's tough to maintain your own emotional state without having another person rub off on you.

Knowing this, it is crucial to regulate our emotions and be aware of how they can impact people, both negatively and positively. What do we bring into each situation at work, at home, and in our friendships? Managing our own emotions is an effective tool to influence other people's moods. I'm not advocating that we manipulate people but rather leverage our emotional state to inspire positive feelings in others.

CALIBRATE YOUR MIND

Reality check from my engineer's perspective: I know that any system operating without a feedback mechanism will eventually drift because it's missing the constant calibration necessary to keep the system accurate. The same happens with our minds. Our emotions arise in response to our thoughts, but no feedback mechanism is built into this process.

We must intentionally add that feedback loop by stepping back and asking ourselves if our thoughts are a reasonable representation of reality and if our emotions are a proportionate and appropriate response. You can see this impact in your own life. Just think about how the same incident affects two people completely differently. One might respond more anxiously, one more calmly. One might react as if it is an emergency, one like it's no big deal at all.

---

36 Reber, *The Penguin Dictionary of Psychology*, s.v. "Contagion, Behavioral (or Emotional)," 158.

Small systemic biases and distortions will creep in and accumulate over time. They might not make much difference at first, but think of what happens after ten or thirty years of never calibrating our minds. Not only do these biases and distortions compound, but we also start labeling them as truth rather than the errors they are.

It's vital to remember that we can train our minds, just like our bodies. Think of professional athletes—gymnasts, for example. They continuously monitor every component of their movements to identify and correct any distortions. It takes precision to land a double backflip perfectly. This relentless calibration process is a matter of life or death for gymnasts because inaccuracy can lead to serious injuries. We can apply this continuous feedback loop to our brains to identify and correct any distortions in our thoughts so our emotional response matches the situation we're facing. It isn't easy to unlearn decades of distorted thinking, but it can be done.

The key is not judging ourselves for the feelings and thoughts we're having right now. Accepting our current state of heart and mind creates the necessary space to learn and make a change.

COMMON THOUGHT DISTORTIONS

The 2010 INSEAD 11 distortion model is a helpful tool for identifying cognitive distortions. My professor, Allan Filipowicz, shared this presentation with our class on Psychological Issues in Management during my MBA program. One of the most easily recognizable distortions is *all-or-nothing thinking*, an extreme polarity of thought. There is no gray area; everything is good or bad, right or wrong. That only works if we're perfect (which we're not), so as soon as we make even one mistake, we're a failure.

Generalization causes us to draw broad conclusions based on a single event. We treat one event as a general rule. Have you ever caught yourself thinking, "I never get that parking spot!" just because you didn't get it on that one visit to the mall? When a new colleague responds with a curt email, we may be more likely to think it's a pattern or a character defect rather than an isolated incident.

Making mountains out of molehills and exaggerating minor problems into catastrophes is called *magnification*. Attaching behaviors to personality types, termed *labeling*, occurs when we turn what someone does into who they are. If you get a bad grade on an exam, you may immediately consider yourself a failure. If you behave unkindly or dishonestly, you may call yourself a terrible person.

Mental filters lead us to ignore the positive information that contradicts a negative opinion we hold. You may tell yourself, "I always procrastinate on big projects," dismissing all of the times you started early and finished on deadline. You might feel the economy is going downhill when statistics show it's trending up, but you refuse to accept this contrary information because it doesn't fit your established ideas.

Do you have a hard time accepting compliments? That could be an example of *discounting the positive*. Say you get praise from your boss for a successful project. You may have difficulty accepting the positive feedback and minimize your success or contribution. You may say the task was easy or unimportant, or start pointing out your mistakes. Our minds are wired to pay more attention to the negative while dismissing the positive.

Jumping to conclusions is prevalent and easy to spot because we all do it frequently. Your client hasn't returned your call? He's probably avoiding you. Your date had to leave early? She doesn't like you. Your coworker was short at the meeting? He has it out for you. We default to a negative interpretation of neutral events. We fail to consider the infinite number of potential reasons that have nothing to do with us. Your client was busy, your date had an early appointment in the morning, and your coworker received terrible health news.

Mind reading is making presumptions about people's thoughts, feelings, or intentions and then basing our own behavior on potentially erroneous ideas. I might presume that my boss thinks I'm incompetent. She's never said this to me, and I've never outright asked her. I made an assumption based on her tone of voice or a statement that sounded passive-aggressive. This is similar to *jumping to conclusions*, but it goes one step further. These unverified opinions then impact our behavior and can become a self-fulfilling prophecy. Because I think my boss believes me to be incompetent, I question my own abilities, get more anxious at work, and make mistakes that my boss notices, reinforcing the whole cycle.

Do you always wait for the other shoe to drop? If you're in the habit of imagining worst-case scenarios, you may be engaging in *crystal ball gazing*. Unfortunately, it's usually adverse future events we predict, such as getting fired at our meeting with the boss tomorrow or getting diagnosed with cancer at our annual checkup.

Be careful if you frequently use *should statements*, which turn preferences into moral imperatives. Pay attention if you often use the words "should," "ought," "have to," or "must." Telling yourself that you "must not mislabel your slides" or "have to be five minutes early for every meeting" can lead to outsized feelings of guilt for not living up to arbitrary standards or making minor errors and common mistakes.

Personalization describes feeling responsible for events out of our control, such as apologizing to a client for an unpredictable market swing. Children often feel responsible for their parents' divorce, thinking there would be no fights or breakups if only they had behaved better.[37]

You've probably recognized yourself in at least a few of these examples. Have you heard the saying "Don't believe everything you think"? It's an excellent approach for dealing with thought distortions. Once we understand that our thoughts aren't facts but hypotheses that can be proven or disproven, it's easier to make it a practice to ask ourselves if any other potential assumptions could apply to a situation.

EXERCISE
Don't Believe Everything You Think

Take a piece of paper and pick a topic (like parenting, money, relationships, or self-improvement, for example). Write down the first ten thoughts that come to your mind.

Don't worry about this too much, and don't edit yourself. Just go with whatever pops into your head. Look at your list of thought distortions and assign them to the statements about your topic. Sometimes more than one distortion may apply to a single statement.

Now reframe your statements into healthier, more reasonable perspectives, and see how that feels. It might be awkward at first because you're not used to it. If you judge yourself harshly, this exercise might feel like making excuses or letting yourself off the hook. If that's the case, try the old trick of pretending you're talking to a good friend or a loved one, then extend that same kindness to yourself.

---

37 American Academy of Child and Adolescent Psychiatry, "Children and Divorce."

For a more personalized exercise, recall a strong emotion you experienced in the last twenty-four hours, instead of picking a random topic. For example, perhaps you were angry because you and your partner forgot to pay the electric bill and now you have been assessed a late fee. So why did you get angry? After all, we're human and sometimes forget to pay a bill.

Ask yourself specifically which thoughts preceded your anger about the event:

- *My partner never pays attention.*
- *I have to do everything, or nothing will get done.*
- *Upstanding people pay their bills on time.*
- *I can't afford that late fee because I also have to get gas to get to work.*

Then reframe the statements:

- *Both of us missed the notice because we've had a lot going on.*
- *Maybe we could try splitting up the bills each of us is responsible for and put them on the calendar.*
- *It's human to forget things. We all have a lot on our minds.*
- *We could ask the company to waive the late fee since it's the first time this has happened and our account is in good standing.*

Pay attention to what happens to your emotions in response to thinking, writing, or speaking aloud your initial statements and your reframed sentences.

REWIRE YOUR BRAIN TO INCREASE YOUR HAPPINESS

I know it may feel silly at first, but the previous exercise is a great way to see the patterns in your thinking. You likely gravitate toward a few thought distortions, while others don't factor heavily into your thinking. The two most important steps are first, correctly identifying our underlying thoughts and ideas before labeling them as specific cognitive distortions; second, reframing them in convincing, realistic, and probable ways. Once we start consistently accepting our negative emotions and thoughts, followed by neutral or positive reframing of these thoughts, we'll see our resulting emotions shift into the positive.

One of my personal Achilles' heels is all-or-nothing thinking. It was especially prevalent in my early twenties, when I was unhappy with my life, my job, my relationships, and mostly, myself. My all-or-nothing thinking made me believe I was a failure because not every aspect of my life was perfect. I magnified every problem and inconvenience and often blamed them on other people. I discounted any positive actions—both my own and other people's—and minimized the importance of my friendships and contributions at work. I was quick to jump to conclusions, expecting the worst of everyone and seeing the world as a harsh and unfair place.

Although identifying your thought patterns and distortions may take a bit of time initially, you are retraining your mind in the process. This practice will help you get better and faster at identifying and reframing your cognitive distortions as they are happening in real time. Don't worry, this won't take months or years to learn. It's not uncommon to see significant changes in a matter of days and weeks.

YOU MAY END UP CHANGING MORE THAN JUST YOUR FEELINGS

Once I distilled my thinking on paper and wrote out the ideas and thoughts that preceded my emotions, it was as if a veil lifted off my eyes. The world looked different. Putting the thoughts on paper allowed me to analyze my ideas rationally. So many of them didn't even make sense. I identified several issues and aspects of my life where my thinking held me back even though I could make positive changes. I quit the job I hated and moved 870 miles away to Houston to start a new career. It was a fresh start for a new chapter in my life.

Sometimes the actions you take will be dramatic, and sometimes they will be much more subtle. Soon you'll experience what it feels like to master situations that used to trigger you. You'll be able to digest complex information without plunging into emotional reactivity. You'll notice that you have a clearer path for navigating future triggers, such as procrastination and *emotional scenario planning* (ruminating on what-if questions). You may have heard of the little procrastination hack I use every day. Whenever I'm about to leave a task for later, I ask myself if it takes less than two minutes. If the answer is yes, I do it right then. These small behavioral changes quickly add up to gaining temporal control of emotional management, one of our most critical abilities to cultivate. Emotional intelligence is one of the keys to healthy relationships, a successful career, and personal peace and clarity. Once you dismantle these cognitive distortions, you will see clearer and realize that the world is much better than you think.

It's important to remember that cognitive distortions happen on a personal micro level as well as on a global macro level. It's easy to be overwhelmed by the negative news in the media because innumerable tragedies and horrors are happening globally at all times. However, the way the media covers negative news also skews our ideas about their frequency and severity—for example, our risk of becoming victims of violent crime or natural disasters. Bad news makes for better ratings than good news. It's no wonder people have no idea how many people have been lifted out of abject poverty, have access to clean drinking water, or improved medical care and nutrition. Additionally, many events happening on a macro level globally do not impact us on a micro level in our country, community, or family. This does not mean that we shouldn't be passionate about the challenges we face together as world citizens, but it does mean that some of our anxiety about our personal lives is misplaced.

In other words, rewiring your brain and reframing your thoughts can lead to more neutral or positive feelings and relief from overwhelm and paralysis so you can act and make positive changes in your life. Of course, there is no way to effect change in yourself without impacting your relationships with others.

YOUR IDEAS ABOUT YOUR KIDS ARE POWERFUL

Learning about this approach to dealing with thoughts and emotions in a healthy way has helped me in my relationships with friends and family but especially with parenting my children. When I became a parent, I tried to prepare myself, talk to people, and read books. In one of these conversations, a friend told me, "Kids will meet their parents' expectations."

Although this sounds like such a simple concept, it is powerful in practice. Our ideas about our kids matter because they produce matching emotions and feelings. Communicating our thoughts to our kids verbally and nonverbally impacts their own ideas and feelings about themselves. Maybe your parents never outright called you stupid, but they made you feel incapable through their actions, looks, or tone of voice. You started thinking that way about yourself, and soon the requisite feelings of anxiety about messing up and thoughts about obsessing over every little mistake crept up.

Our kids will meet our expectations, good or bad. What we believe about them, they will believe about themselves. If we genuinely expect our kids to do well in school, sports, or music, it's much more likely that they will have the confidence to meet those expectations. If we communicate to our children that they can't get things right or typecast them as the problem child, hot mess, or black sheep, they will likely live up to these negative opinions.

I made many mistakes growing up, and luckily, I learned from them. Only the other people involved were my witnesses. Many of these instances are now forgotten and long in the past. For kids in the social media age, every mistake, error in judgment, and indiscretion can become the linchpin that will keep them from their college of choice or dream job. Today, our mistakes live on forever on the internet, reaching not only a few friends or a small community but potentially thousands—or even millions—of total strangers who don't know anything else about us but our worst moments. When every moment, including the ones we're not proud of, is documented, it is much easier to become defined by the worst thing we've done. There is less room for grace and forgiveness and growing up.

On the other hand, this digital scrutiny can lead to people not showing their true selves for fear of being constantly judged and criticized. Social media, in part, is creating a culture in which it is no longer acceptable to make and correct mistakes. Online bullying and public shaming are a reality for this next generation, so their thoughts and emotions are heavily influenced by people whom they have no interaction with in real life. Now more than ever, our kids need us to counteract social media trends of constant criticism and scrutiny. Of course, this does not mean letting them get away with bad behavior or not holding them accountable for their mistakes.

Kids are often more in touch with their emotions than adults and are less likely to repress or mask them. In responding to these often very expressive displays, we can go too far to the extremes. Just like teaching kids to suppress emotions can lead to terrible psychological and physical health outcomes, only validating kids' emotions without teaching them to process these feelings can lead to exaggeration or an unhealthy focus. Ideally, we want to teach kids to identify and feel their emotions, while also encouraging them to ask *why* they feel that way, what's behind the emotion, and which thoughts triggered the feelings in the first place. They will grow up to capably handle their emotions without falling prey to cognitive distortions that paint an inaccurate worldview.

KEY TAKEAWAYS

- Thoughts drive emotions, which, in turn, influence decisions.
- Minor cognitive distortions accumulate over time, causing "system drift" in our brains that we must counteract by consciously recalibrating our thoughts.
- Don't believe everything you think—thoughts aren't facts but hypotheses that can be proven or disproven (Exercise: Don't Believe Everything You Think).

Considering how much our thoughts and emotions influence our inner world, daily life, and most important relationships, isn't it worth the time to learn how to harness the power of our minds?

Investing in this effort now will help fortify you for difficult times ahead that require you to mobilize all of your internal resources.

Chapter 5

BLACK SWANS

> The attempt to escape from pain is what creates more pain.
> **—GABOR MATÉ, PHYSICIAN**

I decided to have my wisdom teeth removed several years ago. They were starting to crowd out a smile that had taken years of braces to straighten in the first place. I found a great oral surgeon with an excellent reputation and great reviews to perform this routine procedure. Everyone I spoke to who'd had their wisdom teeth taken out said it wasn't a big deal. It would, however, be a great excuse to eat as much lemon sorbet as I wanted. Little did I know I would not smile for an entire year after waking up from anesthesia.

The routine surgery left half my face temporarily paralyzed, especially my mouth. I drooled every time I drank or ate anything for nearly two months. My ability to smile didn't fully return for almost a year. I still have a small patch of numbness on my face that feels fake, almost like plastic.

Even a routine procedure can go wrong sometimes because doctors are only human. Maybe my surgeon had a bad day, didn't get enough sleep, or simply made an error. Regardless of the cause, at some point unexpected adversity will inevitably come knocking at each of our doors.

BLACK SWAN EVENTS

A black swan event is an unpredictable and rare occurrence on a personal, communal, or global level, with extreme, wide-ranging, negative consequences. It is often rationalized in hindsight. In the United States, 9/11 is often considered a black swan event. Most people perceived it as a horrible, unexpected event with wide-ranging consequences. It was later the topic of much speculation as people tried to puzzle out why it happened and how it could have been predicted.

Black swan events also occur on a personal level. For example, we may lose a job we thought was solid, be diagnosed with a life-threatening illness even though we were in good health, or have a car accident that changes our life's trajectory.

One of the interesting things about black swan events is that we never think they will happen to us. In our minds, they only happen to other people. Unfortunately, nobody is immune and many events that we consider black swan events are much less rare than we'd like to believe.

What is deemed a black swan event depends on the observer. One such example is the COVID-19 pandemic. Most of us considered it an extremely rare, unpredictable disaster, while many experts have warned of the risk of a global pandemic for years, if not decades. We saw the red flags through smaller viral outbreaks such as swine flu, bird flu, and Ebola. Sometimes a black swan event seems rare and unpredictable because we purposely ignore its possibility. If we dare to shed our cognitive distortions and see the world more clearly, we'll increase our chances of anticipating black swan events and dealing with their fallout more productively.

> **WHAT ARE THE BENEFITS OF MENTALLY PREPARING FOR BLACK SWAN EVENTS?**
>
> - You will learn how to train your mind to process and adapt to personal and global disasters.
> - You will strengthen your internal resources to improve your coping skills in hard times, while increasing your happiness in good times.
> - You will learn about tools and practices to calm your mind like meditation, self-hypnosis, mindfulness, breathwork, and therapy.

In this chapter, we'll discuss the resources and activities that help us walk through hardships and talk about the concept of post-traumatic growth to rebuild our lives after catastrophic events. I'll also share with you a few of my favorite simple exercises to calm and ground myself.

RESPONDING TO BLACK SWAN EVENTS

Hundreds of millions of people were directly affected by the global COVID-19 pandemic. In the blink of an eye, life as we knew it completely changed. Some of these changes affected our everyday lives, like not being able to go outside, meet friends, and enjoy hobbies or entertainment. Others were more serious, like losing jobs or being evicted from homes. And worst, many of us got sick or lost loved ones to the virus. All of our lives were upended somehow, and as I write this book, we are still dealing with the lingering impacts.

COVID-19 had vastly different consequences for different people and businesses. It was the launchpad to build hugely successful companies and send existing businesses like Peloton and Zoom into overdrive or businesses like Amazon exploding into the stratosphere. For some people, it meant suddenly relying on food banks and food stamps to feed their families. Such disparity resulting from a single event is difficult to wrap our minds around.

For many of us, COVID-19 brought with it a mix of negatives and positives. For me, it meant losing a significant investment in my company after spending two years trying to secure it. However, the pandemic also allowed me to spend time with my family and improve my exercise and eating habits. Ultimately, the pandemic was my impetus for slowing down enough to stop the unending rush of life, reflect on my goals, and get clear on what truly mattered to me.

We quickly take our life for granted and forget how much even a significant loss hurt us in the past. Lockdowns were an interesting example of that. Did you dream about the smallest things that signified normalcy? Did you envision hugging your grandma, smiling at someone in the grocery store, standing in line at the movies, or having a drink with a friend? And if you've been able to experience some of these small joys again as regulations have relaxed, are you still as grateful for them as you thought you would be? Do they still make you as happy now as they did when your community first started opening up?

Training ourselves to remember the times when everything changed instantly is good preparation for when it inevitably happens again. Complex, mentally, and emotionally challenging days are still ahead for all of us, ready to test us and threaten to rob us of every last bit of happiness and satisfaction. Instead of ignoring or denying this reality, we need to prepare ourselves now by strengthening our emotional and mental capacity. Building up our resilience ahead of time will allow us to better manage whatever challenge may come our way.

NAVIGATING THROUGH LIFE'S DIFFICULTIES

It is entirely normal and necessary to feel sadness, anger, grief, loss, and disappointment when bad things happen to us or the people we love the most. Although we may look back on these situations with a deeper understanding in the future, living through them fully in the moment is the basis on which any future wisdom must be built. I've made many mistakes in the midst of trying to deal with the losses in my own life. I've tried to rush the grieving process and glossed over the pain. It's tempting to reach for closure and distilled wisdom without truly feeling the pain life brings and allowing our minds the time necessary to grapple with our new reality.

A friend of my mother's lost her seven-year-old child. She said, "I've already experienced the worst thing possible for a parent. That pain is never going away. And yet, I'm still alive. There are things I want to do with my life and things I want to contribute to this world." Some pains will stay with us forever, but we can continue to live alongside the pain. It doesn't have to be one or the other: we don't have to try and make the pain disappear before we can live again or decide to give up and not live at all. So much of life is figuring out how to do both—accept the pain into our lives without letting it keep us from living.

As we discussed in Chapter 2, grief is one of those complex processes that is never done and will remain with us throughout our lives. Although Chapter 2 focused on how to process hard times in our past, this chapter is about fortifying ourselves for current and future hardships.

In addition to committing to regular therapy for several years now, I'm leaning heavily on simple daily tools to help me process life's difficulties as they arise. I've found a helpful combination for me is to work through serious issues in therapy and practice quick and easy calming and grounding techniques such as breathwork and mindfulness throughout the day. The main idea I want you to take away is that there is no one magic bullet for dealing with difficult parts of your life and that you can mix and match different resources and activities. I have found it most helpful to be open to support regardless of origin.

When I was seventeen, I developed ulcers caused by a bacterial infection, which required me to take medicine to protect my gastric tube. I took medication for twenty years and rarely thought about it, although I regularly experienced significant side effects like extreme heartburn and the probability of decreased bone density in the future. My wife encouraged me to seek natural ways to help my body in addition to medication, so I signed up for an Ayurveda class. As a result, I eliminated spicy foods from my diet (not an easy feat with Mexican cuisine), which alleviated my symptoms significantly. Today, I no longer have to take my medication. I'm able to manage my symptoms solely through dietary changes. I'm not a doctor, and I'm not advocating for anyone going off medication. However, I want to invite you to consider that there is always more than one option that might help you, give you relief, or support you in feeling better.

Breathing is one of the easiest and simplest methods to calm your body and mind. We often overlook its importance because it feels basic and automatic. Combined with a quick grounding exercise, I use conscious breathing on a daily basis. Following are a few techniques you can try out and incorporate into your customized daily routine.

EXERCISE
Breathwork and Grounding Technique

In the Ayurveda class, I learned a breathing technique that I use to this day, which has helped me immensely in calming my body and mind. The course encouraged me to slow down, listen to my body, learn mindfulness, and incorporate simple practices to ground myself in the present moment. I practice these tools every day, especially when facing a stressful event, emotionally difficult situation, or mentally challenging day. The following breathing exercise and mindfulness technique are two quick ideas you can try out right now.

Breathing Exercise
Breathe in for three counts, hold for three counts, breathe out for three counts. Repeat five times.

In the Ayurveda class, I was instructed to practice this every day for six months with the goal of breathing in for one minute, holding for one minute, and breathing out for two minutes. I never got to that goal and didn't find it practical or helpful for me. I took the freedom to experiment with this breathing exercise until I landed on what works for me. Nothing is set in stone. I've settled on 5-5-5, breathing in for five counts, holding for five, and breathing out for five.

Another variation of this exercise is box breathing, where you add a hold after the exhale.

Breathe in for five counts, hold for five, exhale for five, hold for five, and start again.

Grounding Exercise

Take a deep breath. Look around you and name:

5-4-3-2-1 TECHNIQUE

You might have seen this graphic or similar ones floating around online. I recently tried out this grounding technique on a day when I was running to back-to-back important meetings. I first used my breathing technique to calm myself and then used the grounding exercise to focus on my physical experience and clear my mind of distracting thoughts. To remember the grounding exercise, set an alarm on your phone, or tape a Post-it-note to your wall, mirror, or desktop, I've found the practice to be easily incorporated into my day.

You can do this exercise wherever you are. Just follow the prompts:

- Find five things you can see, such as the blue sky through your office window, a ring on your finger, or a favorite picture on your desk.

- Then focus on four things you can feel or touch: the soft sweater you're wearing, the waxy leaf of a potted plant, or the warm mug of coffee in your hand.

- Next, listen to three things you can hear like your coworkers laughing in the hallway, a plane flying overhead, or an insect buzzing.

- Now identify two things you can smell, maybe the coffee in your mug or the fresh blooms on your plant.
- Finally, focus on one thing you can taste, whether it's your coffee breath or the minty piece of gum you just popped in your mouth.

The exercise works whether the sensory experiences are negative or positive. In other words, it doesn't matter if your sweater is soft or scratchy, whether the sounds are pleasant or annoying, or if you're in a beautiful or bland environment. The point is paying attention to your sensory experience, which grounds you in the present.

POST-TRAUMATIC GROWTH

Hard times that cause pain and suffering come for all of us, but I have seen in my own life and with many of my friends and family that difficulties also bring growth, wisdom, and deeper joy. As I've watched my mother go through brain cancer surgery, treatments, and rehabilitation, I've been inspired by her tenacity. As a young girl and throughout her adult years, one of my mother's greatest passions has been dancing. She even performed on stage with a dance troupe. Before her diagnosis, she still danced as a hobby and made friends with other women from her community dance class. One day, my mother's physical therapist decided to mix up the session by adding some much needed fun and social support. As a surprise, the physical therapist invited some of my mother's dance friends and they all spent the session dancing together.

Perhaps you've heard of the concept of post-traumatic growth (PTG) as developed by psychologists Richard Tedeschi and Lawrence Calhoun in the mid-'90s. Tedeschi and Calhoun used a self-report scale, the Post-traumatic Growth Inventory (PTGI), to evaluate people after they went through significant personal challenges.[38] For my mother, PTG wasn't simply regaining her physical abilities after surgery but reconnecting with her friends, reigniting her passion for dance, and finding new hope in rebuilding her life. Tedeschi and Calhoun found that about half to two-thirds of people show PTG after enduring the psychological struggle that comes with facing adversity. Specifically, they found people showed improvement and progress across the following five primary domains.

APPRECIATION FOR LIFE

The adage of *not knowing what we got till it's gone* is true insofar as that the threat of loss makes us more grateful for what we have. Even if we lose something or someone significant, that loss can spur greater thankfulness for what and who remains. We generally become better at noticing the little things that make life beautiful, pleasurable, and happy. Understanding that life, health, and happiness are not guaranteed and are rather fragile makes it all more precious.

RELATIONSHIPS WITH OTHERS

Hard times can improve our relationships in different ways. We may realize that we can depend on the people closest to us, sparking profound gratitude and increased closeness. Giving and getting support fosters close bonds—at least in healthy relationships. We may also choose to terminate relationships with unsupportive or actively damaging people, while striking up new connections with like-minded people who have been through similar experiences.

---

38 Collier, "Growth after Trauma," 48.

NEW POSSIBILITIES

Sometimes trauma forces us to stop what we're doing and how we've always done it. We may need to consider new habits and strategies to survive. However, a change in perspective may also create new possibilities, ideas, and desires we didn't know existed. We might find a new passion, change our careers, leave an unhealthy relationship, connect with an old friend, or start a new habit.

PERSONAL STRENGTH

You might be surprised at how well you handled the curveball life threw at you. You may notice increased confidence and trust in yourself after you make it through an intense struggle. You are now more equipped to tackle future hardships with the knowledge that you survived the last one.

SPIRITUAL CHANGE

You don't have to become a believer or join a church, but our most difficult times often involve asking ourselves probing questions: *Why am I here? What do I want to do with my life? What matters to me?* These questions and our answers might change our outlook on life, our philosophy, morality, or ethics. We may find or lose religion, or develop a new understanding of spirituality, transcendence, and life's purpose. In the face of near-insurmountable challenges, we must find a reason to keep going and design a life worth living.

Considering the five domains of PTG, it's important to remember that growth happens gradually and often imperceptibly. It can't be rushed. Jumping immediately to the possibility of growth in the middle of a difficult time can lead to minimizing our pain or that of others. Growth, in other words, is a by-product of facing and processing the challenge and being patient with ourselves.

According to Tedeschi, the personality traits of openness and extraversion make people more likely to experience PTG because these individuals are more likely to reconsider their beliefs and more comfortable seeking out resources and human connections in response to their trauma. The graphic below illustrates the impact of PTG on an individual's life.

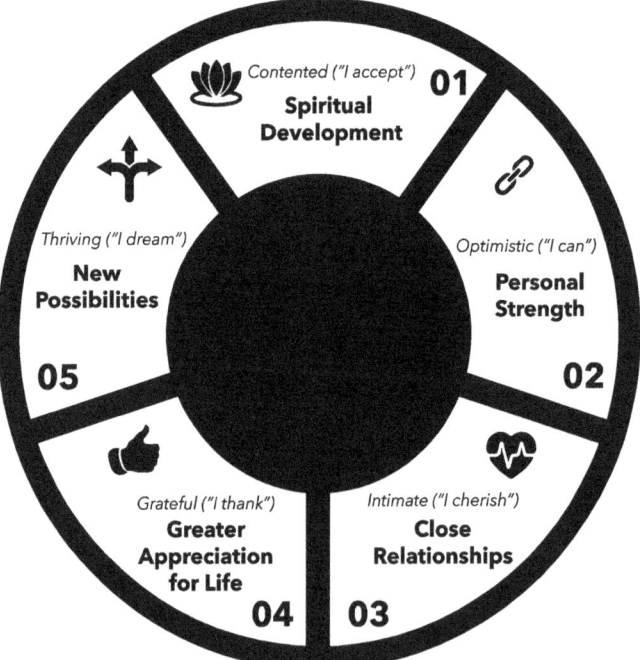

5 Domains of Post-Traumatic Growth

01 — **"Out of spiritual doubt there can emerge a deeper faith"**

- **Change Catalyst**: Deeper cognitive engagement with fundamental existential questions about death and the purpose of life
- **Recognition**: Presence of higher power
- **Wisdom**: We are not alone
- **Improved Qualities**: Fully developed and meaningful beliefs and philosophies of life, deeper level of awareness, deeper faith in the divine
- **Positive Coping Mechanism**: Meditation, prayer and conection to self and a higher presence

02 — **"At a time when one is vulnerable as never before, there is a sense of strength"**

- **Change Catalyst**: Reflection on personal strength demonstrated through adversities
- **Recognition**: Greater sense of personal strength to handle blows in life
- **Wisdom**: Adversities are inevitable in human life
- **Improved Qualities**: Resilience, self-reliance, maturity to accept outcomes, meaningful and coherent trauma narrative
- **Positive Coping Mechanism**: Remaining positive, seeking meaning, and exploring ways to reduce emotional distress

03 — **"Some deeper relationships form while losing others"**

- **Change Catalyst**: Seeking connection and support with authentic sharing
- **Recognition**: Acceptance of needing others
- **Wisdom**: Discernment of true friends
- **Improved Qualities**: Intimacy in relationships, increased emotional vulnerability, loving and empathetic, sense of belonging
- **Positive Coping Mechanism**: Reaching out to others

04 — **"What can break us open can also open us more to life"**

- **Change Catalyst**: Upheaval in major assumptions about the world and one's place in it
- **Recognition**: Value of life and importance of little things
- **Wisdom**: Small joys in life are not to be taken for granted
- **Improved Qualities**: Sense of priorities, gratitude, being in the present moment, altruism
- **Positive Coping Mechanism**: Deeper contemplation for value and meaning

05 — **"Out of loss there can be gain"**

- **Change Catalyst**: Acceptance of the breakage and formulation of revised goals in the changed life circumstances
- **Recognition**: Availability of new opportunities and reframed purpose of life
- **Wisdom**: The serenity to accept the things that one cannot change, the courage to change the things one can, and the wisdom to know the difference
- **Improved Qualities**: New interests, new perspective, adaptability, openness to new ways of living
- **Positive Coping Mechanism**: Buoyant pursuit of new fulfilling paths

Although you can gain PTG through therapy, there are also other ways to progress through the framework that Tedeschi and Calhoun proposed—namely, education, emotional regulation, disclosure, narrative development, and acts of service. In a 2021 *Harvard Business Review* article, Tedeschi provided helpful explanations for how to utilize these five approaches to increase PTG.[39]

EDUCATION

Tedeschi explains that "to move through trauma to growth, one must first get educated about what the former is: a disruption of core belief systems. For example, before the pandemic, many of us thought we were safe from the types of diseases that endangered people in the past; that bad things happened in other parts of the world but not ours; and that our social and economic systems were resilient enough to weather all storms. None of that was true. So now we need to figure out what to believe instead."[40]

When we go through personal or collective trauma, the resulting fear can produce crippling anxiety and intrusive repetitive thoughts about why something happened to us and what we should do next. It's painful to see our assumptions disproven. It's difficult to challenge our own narratives about the world, who we are as people, and what our future will hold. But no matter how hard, educating ourselves on our new reality is paramount.

EMOTIONAL REGULATION

Tedeschi reminds us of the concepts we discussed in Chapter 4 and their influence on our feelings. We can only learn when we are in the right frame of mind, which "starts with managing

---

39 Tedeschi, "Growth after Trauma."
40 Tedeschi, "Growth after Trauma."

negative emotions such as anxiety, guilt, and anger, which can be done by shifting the kind of thinking that leads to those feelings. Instead of focusing on losses, failures, uncertainties, and worst-case scenarios, try to recall successes, consider best-case possibilities, reflect on your own or your organization's resources and preparation, and think reasonably about what you—personally and as a group—can do…You can regulate emotions directly by observing them as they are experienced."[41]

Tedeschi further shares advice on how physical exercise, breathing practices, and meditation also help regulate emotions. We've already discussed some of these tools, and we'll continue our conversation in Chapter 6.

DISCLOSURE

I've personally felt the healing effects of being open with a few trustworthy people in my life, especially my wife. According to Tedeschi, disclosure is a vital step to PTG because articulating our past and ongoing challenges "helps us to make sense of the trauma and turn debilitating thoughts into more-productive reflections."[42]

Opening up about my own struggles helped me tremendously and affected the people around me. If I was vulnerable enough to speak truthfully, the other person was more likely to respond similarly, leading to greater intimacy, understanding, and trust in our relationship and a collective feeling of unburdening. As Tedeschi says, the disclosure isn't merely a relief but also helps us with sense making and reframing what has happened to us so we can better integrate it into our lives.

---

41 Tedeschi, "Growth after Trauma."
42 Tedeschi, "Growth after Trauma."

NARRATIVE DEVELOPMENT

Disclosure is the first step in creating a congruent story about your trauma: "How has it caused you to recalibrate your priorities? What new paths or opportunities have emerged from it?" are two questions Tedeschi suggests we ask ourselves. The goal is to develop "an authentic narrative about the trauma and our lives afterward so that we can accept the chapters already written and imagine crafting the next ones in a meaningful way."[43]

This ties back to what we discussed about accepting our past and history so that we can make decisions about our future in Chapter 2. Narrative development isn't about slapping a cheap moral on our life story but genuinely considering if the challenge or trauma has caused our priorities to shift, changed beliefs about ourselves or the world, or given us glimpses of hope in unexpected places.

ACTS OF SERVICE

Although it's not advisable to rush out and focus on everyone else to distract yourself from feeling the pain of your own hardship while you're still neck-deep in it, there is healing in reaching out to others. However, it is essential to go slow and not overdo it. "People do better in the aftermath of trauma if they find work that benefits others—helping people close to them or their broader community or victims of events similar to the ones they have endured."

Tedeschi echoes the desire of many people to turn their pain into relief for others. "Of course," he says, "you don't need to start a nonprofit or a foundation to be of service." Acts of service can

---

[43] Tedeschi, "Growth after Trauma."

be as simple as expressing gratitude and compassion to others in your daily life, volunteering, or donating to causes you care about. Most importantly, Tedeschi says, "Look for personal and shared missions that energize you and help you find meaning."[44]

MY PERSONAL EXPERIENCE WITH POST-TRAUMATIC GROWTH

I experienced PTG in my own life primarily through a new and different appreciation for life and a reinforced belief in my personal strength. Going through some of my personal challenges, like losing my friend Richard and my mentor Joe, watching my mother's struggle with a brain tumor, or my mother-in-law's ALS battle, showed me that life was precious and fragile. Those of us who were left behind were much more resilient than I thought. We came together when life threatened to break us apart. When everything got terribly hard, we leaned on each other and found deep wells of strength within ourselves. I found renewed conviction that I could pull through and come out the other side.

PTG also changed my close relationships, especially with my wife and kids, parents and siblings, and close friends. My relationships have deepened and solidified as I've learned to open up and be more comfortable with being vulnerable. I'm more present with my kids; I have improved the quality of our time together and am more curious about who they are becoming. Therapy and the resulting PTG have allowed me to create more intimacy, trust, and understanding in my marriage.

PTG can have a profound impact on our spiritual development. I grew up in a Catholic family, and faith has always been important

---

44 Tedeschi, "Growth after Trauma."

to me. I try to learn from my Jewish and Muslim friends as much as I can, knowing that often it is the institutions and extremists that are the problem, not individual people's faith. While PTG has fortified my Catholic faith, it has also encouraged me to seek truth, wisdom, and goodness from all my friends and loved ones who belong to different cultures and faith traditions.

When exploring new possibilities, some people start charities or become public advocates for causes near to their hearts after going through intense personal struggles. They desire to share their wisdom, resources, and experience, connect with people who are suffering, or drive societal change. This is one reason why I decided to write this book. Since I was young, I've been practical and logical to a fault, sometimes to the point of seeming a little too cool, calm, and collected. However, that part of my personality drew in my friends during their most challenging times. I was the go-to guy, not for recommendations on the best tennis racket to buy but the friend you went to when your wife just told you she wanted a divorce. My house and my arms have always been open to the people I care about at their lowest points and worst moments. Of course, this doesn't mean that I haven't experienced my own rock-bottom situations or that I always know what to say or do. However, many of my friends have told me they appreciate my approach to life and its joys and difficulties. I've shared my experiences and resources with them as an invitation to experiment, rather than rigid advice or one-size-fits-all prescriptions. Now I hope this book will do the same for you.

> **KEY TAKEAWAYS**
>
> - We can't spend our time worrying about *what* might happen, but we need to accept that things *will* happen.
> - You are tougher than you think.
> - You can adapt to adversity and grow from it.
> - Strengthen your mind in daily practice such as mindfulness, breathwork, or therapy to be as prepared as possible (Exercise: Breathwork and Grounding Technique).

During the pandemic, we all had to adjust to a new reality. It wasn't easy, but we did it. Whether dealing with personal or global black swan events, building up our internal resources is critical. This book has been a way for me to organize my thoughts and share what has helped me: the tools, activities, exercises, techniques, and resources that make me stronger and happier.

Next I will share some research findings about what makes us happy and how to incorporate more happiness-inducing activities and habits into our daily lives.

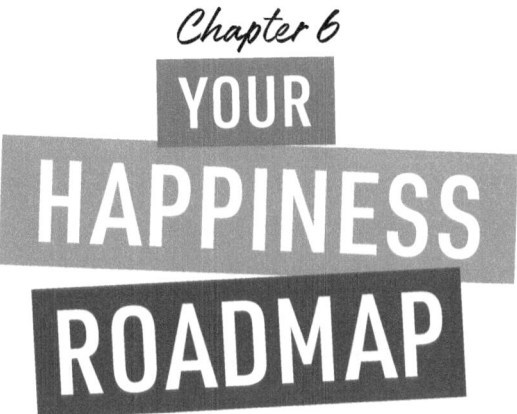

Chapter 6
YOUR HAPPINESS ROADMAP

> Absorb what is useful, discard what is useless,
> and add what is specifically your own.
> **—BRUCE LEE, MARTIAL ARTIST**

It had been three long, miserable days, and I was still hungover. Although it wasn't unusual for me to party until four or five in the morning several times a week during college, I'd never been blackout drunk and hungover for days. I had no memory of the night that got me here, but unfortunately, my friends did. I was ashamed of the things I'd said and done. I didn't want to be the kind of person who'd completely lose control of their mind and body. I needed a big change but didn't know where to start, so I took a drastic first step. I quit drinking for an entire year.

Being completely sober helped my body feel better after I'd tortured it with excessive alcohol consumption and sleep deprivation for years. My mind also started healing, feeling clearer and calmer. I experienced a new peace. Although quitting alcohol was a dramatic step, it wasn't the first or last on my continuing journey with happiness (not *to* happiness). I've learned that happiness is not the destination but how I walk the road. Some of the steps I took seemed extreme to others, but I had to trust myself to know what was right for me. I had to repeat some steps multiple times. Some were small, and a few took me down a side path that led nowhere. In other words, I'm still taking it step by step and course correcting as needed.

In this chapter, I'll share my roadmap with you and invite you to forge your own path. Creating a happier life spans every aspect of our physical and mental health, relationships with friends and family, work and finances, activities and hobbies, contribution to the community, and our legacy. Some of these parts of life are universal. For example, research I'll share with you in this chapter shows that significant predictors of happiness include the quality of our relationships and meaningful contributions to our communities. Some are unique to our specific lives and personalities, such as the things we love to do for their own sake. Creative pursuits, sports, and learning new skills all allow us to fully immerse ourselves and forget time entirely.

Too often, we hear self-proclaimed experts, books, podcasts, articles, or celebrities focus on one aspect, one activity, one tool, or one behavior to increase happiness at the expense of everything else. But often, it is a cluster of behaviors, activities, or resources that, taken together, affect our happiness but do little individually. Additionally, as with lots of research, the relationship between happiness and our efforts to improve it is usually a correlation, rarely causation.

> **WHAT ARE THE BENEFITS OF LOOKING AT HAPPINESS HOLISTICALLY?**
>
> - You will understand how different areas of your life impact your happiness.
> - You will reflect on the areas of your life that are currently holding you back from being as happy as possible.
> - You will realize which sustainable changes and consistent habits you can implement to add more happiness to your life.

This chapter digs into how the parts that make up our lives contribute or take away from our happiness and what we can do about it. There is no one-size-fits-all approach to overhauling and fixing every aspect of your life to reach peak happiness 24/7. However, we can reflect on our lives, experiences, and relevant research to make meaningful change that results in greater satisfaction and happiness.

HOW MAJOR LIFE AREAS AFFECT HAPPINESS

Health (nutrition, exercise, sleep, stress management, nature), relationships (romantic love, family and parenting, friends), work (career fulfillment and money), personal growth (learning, giving, hobbies, goals), and purpose (spirituality and faith) all significantly impact our life satisfaction and happiness. I'm not suggesting you completely overhaul every part of your life, but I want to provide some ideas for small changes in each area that can make a big difference.

HEALTH

Without question, health is one of the most critical parts of our life, and it's also notoriously taken for granted. We often don't consciously care for our bodies until we have an accident or are diagnosed with an illness. Food, exercise, and sleep are the most vital areas we need to improve to elevate our health and happiness. It often feels like a chicken or egg situation in which health and happiness affect each other so profoundly that it's challenging to figure out which one comes first. Research has found a correlation between happiness and longevity, showing that happy people live longer and that feelings of positive affect can even lower inflammation markers.[45] Of course, one measure of a happy life is not its length but its quality, and taking care of our health is one surefire way to improve the quality of our experiences.

One of my favorite books about nutrition, exercise, and rest is *Power of 10* by Adam Zickerman.[46] I've found this book incredibly helpful and straightforward, and I will share my experiences implementing its advice in the following pages. However, any health-related changes you want to make should be discussed with your physician and fit your specific circumstances and health concerns.

NUTRITION

Food has the power to make you happy. About 95 percent of serotonin, a happy hormone, is made in our guts. Researchers are still trying to figure out exactly how our nutrition affects this hormone's production, but we've got some exciting clues. A 2014

---

45 Lawrence, Rogers, and Wadsworth, "Happiness and Longevity," 115–119; Stellar et al., "Positive Affect and Inflammation," 129–133.
46 Zickerman and Schley, *Power of 10: The Once-a-Week Slow Motion Fitness Revolution.*

study in the *American Journal of Clinical Nutrition* analyzed twenty-one nutritional studies. Although randomized controlled trials and cohort studies are needed to prove causation, there are strong correlations between whole foods nutrition and happiness. The results suggest that "high intakes of fruit, vegetables, fish, and whole grains may be associated with a reduced depression risk."[47] One study showed that women who eat a Mediterranean diet of fruits, vegetables, whole grains, and fish were 17 percent less likely to experience depressive symptoms than people who ate SAD (standard American diet) full of red meat, fried foods, and dairy.[48]

I don't believe in short-term fad diets or the idea that there is a one-size-fits-all approach. My father, who is a physician, always told me, "I don't treat diseases. I treat patients." We're all different, and we need to know ourselves well enough to discuss the best way to eat for our optimal personal health with our doctors. For example, several studies in the United States and Finland have shown that coffee consumption correlated with a decreased risk for depression and suicidal ideation.[49] However, most of these studies only included female participants, so it's possible the results can't be extrapolated to men. Many people report digestive issues or increased anxiety when consuming too much coffee, and caffeine consumption can be problematic for certain health issues and chronic illnesses. In other words, what may be great for one person may be harmful to the next. It's essential to pay attention to our body, talk with our doctor, and get expert advice.

---

47 Lai et al., "Dietary Patterns and Depression," 181.
48 Rienks et al., "Mediterranean Dietary Pattern and Prevalence," 75–82.
49 Lucas et al., "Coffee, Caffeine, and Depression," 1571–1578.

STOP JUDGING YOURSELF FOR A LACK OF "SELF-CONTROL"

Even though experts disagree on the finer points, we all know the main guidelines for good nutrition. We make things more complicated than they need to be when the truth is, we all know the choice is clear when it comes to deciding between a bag of chips and a piece of fruit. The more significant issue for me wasn't understanding what foods were good for me but how to consistently *make* these healthier choices. I was surrounded by fast food on my drive home, junk food in my pantry, and office snacks at work.

One of Zickerman's central ideas is the "cheat day" during which you can eat whatever you want. For me, it's easier to stick to mostly healthy foods during the week if I know that I'll be able to indulge in my cravings once a week. Giving in to cravings once in a while actually helps us make better choices over time. Adam Drewnowski, a researcher at the University of Washington who focuses on food and taste, explains that "dietary restrictions definitely make cravings worse."[50]

Still, how you handle those cravings depends on your personal level of control once you dig into that chocolate cake. Drewnowski clarifies that if you can satisfy your cravings with "a few chocolate Kisses or a fun-size Snickers bar...go for it" but warns that cravings can get out of control.[51]

If you're worried you'll eat the entire cake on your cheat day, it's better to buy portion-controlled treats that are easy to find at grocery stores or restaurants. You can purchase single slices of cake or a serving of fried chicken instead of an entire cake or a family-size bucket. Drewnowski agrees that the point is not to

---

50 Magee, "Facts about Food Cravings."
51 Magee, "Facts about Food Cravings."

judge ourselves for lack of self-control but to focus on changing our environment. You can choose not to keep your candy kryptonite in the cupboard or buy single servings of treats instead of party-size bags.[52]

BORROWING FROM THE JAPANESE

Additionally, I've adapted the Japanese engineering principle of *poka-yoke* to hack my food choices. Poka-yoke stands for the "mistake-proofing" or "inadvertent error prevention" used in industrial engineering processes, but it also applies to how I think about my health choices. I set myself up for success by circumventing bad decisions before they happen.

Since I was little, I've had a sweet tooth. As an adult, my pantry used to be stocked with my favorite snack foods like jalapeño cheese, salt and vinegar chips, and different kinds of cookies and chocolate, especially KitKats and Whatchamacallit bars. Once a craving hit, it was extremely difficult not to walk the few steps to my pantry and pick from the assortment of treats readily available to me. Today, instead of relying on my willpower and decision-making skills, I've made it as easy as possible to make better choices more often. As a family, we stopped buying junk food to keep in the house. Instead, we stock up on our favorite fruit, like strawberries and grapes. Now when I have a sweet tooth, I'm much more likely to grab a handful of strawberries than to put on my shoes and drive to the store to buy chocolate. There are still times when I have a craving strong enough that I'll go out and buy it, but more frequently, I have a piece of fruit, and the urge eventually subsides.

---

52 Magee, "Facts about Food Cravings."

Poka-yoke helped me frame my sweet tooth not as a personal weakness I had to overcome with an iron will but more as a challenge I need to solve to set myself up for success. On days when I make poor food choices and want to judge myself, I remind myself of research showing that our brains are telling us to eat high-fat, high-sugar foods: "For many of us, cravings kick into high gear when we're stressed or anxious. Carbohydrates boost our levels of the hormone serotonin, which has a calming effect. And recent research suggests that the combination of fat and sugar may also have a calming effect."[53]

In other words, when we're stressed out, our brains crave foods high in carbs, sugar, and fat because they (temporarily) make us feel better and calm us down. Reducing stress will therefore reduce cravings, too.

EXERCISE

In addition to our nutritional choices, exercise is a significant health and happiness enhancer, boosting mood and cognitive function while decreasing stress. A study in the journal *Brain Plasticity* explains the benefits of exercise are derived from the increased release of happy hormones, such as dopamine, serotonin, and endorphins.[54]

However, the specific exercise regimens that are considered all the rage change frequently. We must move our bodies regularly, but it matters less how we choose to do it. Maybe you're a person who naturally loves to exercise. More power to you! I'm not like that. I had to slowly build up the habit over time, gradually increasing the intensity and duration of my workouts. Doing

---

53 Magee, "Facts about Food Cravings."
54 Basso and Suzuki, "Effects of Acute Exercise," 127–152.

too much too fast often results in giving up altogether, especially if we overdo it to the point of injury. Taking small steps that I can consistently maintain is worth more than going hard for a short while and then stopping only to restart the cycle again in a few weeks.

Zickerman suggests adding one or two weight training sessions a week, between twenty and twenty-five minutes each. His method consists of extremely slow movements for very few repetitions until muscle failure.[55] His approach worked great for me, but it's not for everyone. I lost more than twenty pounds over six months and have kept the weight off for fifteen years. I've also tried out different exercise programs, such as TRX for body weight workouts, and have trained with free weights. I alternate between a few different types of exercise I enjoy. Mixing up my workouts also helps me stave off boredom—another major reason for quitting. At the same time, jumping on every new and trendy workout class isn't necessary.

Hold yourself accountable, but build in some flexibility to ward off perfectionism. If you miss a workout, start again the next day instead of telling yourself it's all over because you messed up your perfect streak.

SLEEP

Studies extolling the virtues of sleep and rest and their impact on our overall health are too numerous to count. A UK study showed a correlation between longer and better sleep and less sleep medication use with increased well-being. Although this study doesn't prove a causal relationship, the self-reported results of over

---

[55] Zickerman and Schley, *Power of 10: The Once-a-Week Slow Motion Fitness Revolution*.

30,000 participants show that an improvement in sleep impacted psychological well-being and happiness as much as completing an eight-week program of mindfulness-based cognitive therapy or winning a quarter-million dollars in the lottery.[56]

We need sleep to recover physically but also mentally and emotionally. I love the book *Why We Sleep* by neuroscientist and psychologist Matthew Walker, which explains the science behind sleeping and dreaming and how it affects every aspect of our lives.[57] According to Walker, sleep's main benefits on our cognition are improved memory, motor task proficiency or muscle memory, and improved creativity. Aside from the cognitive benefits, Walker claims that research in his sleep lab at the University of California, Berkeley has demonstrated that good sleep provides "overnight therapy" by integrating difficult emotional experiences from the day before. As Walker shared in an interview, experiments in his sleep lab have also shown improvement in mental illnesses and emotional regulation, and enhancement of personal relationships.[58]

It has become somewhat of a badge of honor in our culture, especially in entrepreneurial circles, to boast about sleeping only a few hours every night. Although a small fraction of the population can get by on little sleep, most of us need much more rest than we're currently getting to be at our best. Stanford University professor Baba Shiv explains the importance of deep sleep for recharging our minds and bodies.[59] Shiv recommends at least 7.5 hours of sleep to ideally allow for five full sleep cycles of ninety minutes each. The first three cycles lasting about 4.5 hours are

---

56 Tang et al., "Changes in Sleep," 6–7.
57 Walker, *Why We Sleep.*
58 Suttie, "Sleep Your Way to the Top."
59 Shiv, "Breakthrough Ideas."

especially crucial. The deep or slow wave sleep phases are necessary to help our bodies produce serotonin, which not only helps our moods but also makes the morning the ideal time for decision making. As our serotonin levels decrease over the course of the day, it's harder to make decisions and more likely that you will be indecisive or make decisions based on fear. Shiv also talks about reframing your day before you go to bed because sleep integrates your day's experiences into memory. Frame your daily peak experiences as wins in your mind before going to sleep, and reframe the low points as learning experiences so they don't stick in your long-term memory as losses.

Sleep Routines and Hygiene

No need to overcomplicate things. Specific sleep routines and hygiene have gained popularity, but they can be as involved or simple as is practical for you. Walker, similarly to Shiv, recommends that we should aim for seven hours a night at minimum. Of course, the quality of our sleep also makes a big difference. Take into account your personal preferences, specific life stage, and circumstances. Personally, I don't use my phone in the hour before I go to bed. I also stop drinking coffee and other stimulants, such as caffeinated soda, energy drinks, and tea by 6:00 p.m. I don't eat anything sweet after that time either. This is because sugar acts as a stimulant for our brains, so I have a much harder time falling asleep after eating sweets late at night.

Whether you like it ice cold or warm in your bedroom, pitch black or sleep with your shades open, white noise or not, hard or soft mattress is up to you and will require some experimentation. Depending on your life stage, you may have to coordinate and compromise with your bedmate. If you have small kids as I do, you may not be able to have your preferred sleep schedule for a few years. I like to go to bed and wake up very early, but currently, our kids have a hard time going down at night and often wake up multiple times, coming to us because they're thirsty or scared. My wife and I need to get every minute of sleep that we can in the morning hours because we're up later into the night with kids wandering into our bedroom. The point is to do the best with whatever current situation you're in at any given moment. And if you happen to be in a phase of life similar to mine, know that this time won't last forever, and you can adapt your sleep schedule when circumstances change.

STRESS MANAGEMENT

As we all know by now, stress negatively impacts happiness, but somehow as a society, we still struggle with implementing effective ways to consistently manage that stress. I've shared different activities that can help with stress, such as breathing, meditation, therapy, exercise, and reaching out to loved ones. One specific tool I've used since I was a little child and haven't shared with you yet is self-hypnosis.

Self-hypnosis

I've never been hypnotized by a therapist or any other person for that matter, and I personally wouldn't want to put myself in someone else's hands like that. Not because I believe hypnotherapists are malicious but because I want full control over what happens while I'm in a highly suggestive state. Many of the books I've read on the topic make hypnosis sound much more complicated than what I've experienced it to be. Instead, I've used a simple technique my mother taught me when I was nine years old. I've used it ever since and find it much more straightforward than the approaches I've seen explained in books.

Self-hypnosis helps manage stress through deep physical and mental relaxation. This is the way I do it, as taught to me by my mother.

Step 1: Relaxation

Lie down comfortably and close your eyes. Take three slow, deep breaths. Imagine yourself melting into the mattress or floor. Actively tense and relax each of your muscle groups from top to bottom or bottom to top. For three breaths, feel your legs relax, then take three more breaths for your arms, chest, and shoulders to relax. Finally, take another three breaths to relax your head and neck. Imagine your body so heavy that it is making an indentation below you. Some people may imagine sinking through the floor, descending on an escalator, stairs, or elevator.

Step 2: Instructions

Tell yourself in your head (not out loud) that you will count to three and enter your focus state. Give yourself instructions for what will happen in that focused state before actually counting to three. For example, back when I was a student, I would tell myself that in my focus state, I would know that I was well prepared for my exam, that I would remember everything I studied, and that I would ace the exam. Today, it might be a work meeting or something as simple as telling myself that I will return to a state of calm and gratitude after a particularly emotionally stressful day.

Step 3: Focus State

Then instruct yourself about the cue that will take you out of your focus state. I usually snap my fingers to cue my brain to leave the focus state. You could also use a timer on your phone and instruct yourself that you'll leave the focus state once you hear the alarm go off. You might tell your brain to exit the focus state a certain period of time after entering it without a specific cue. Only after you've given yourself all the instructions about what will happen in your focus state and when you will exit, count to three to allow yourself to enter the focus state.

There, you will address the issue per your previous instructions or the reason for the hypnosis, and once your cue alerts you, you will exit the focus state.

Are You Scared of Self-hypnosis?

Contrary to popular belief, you can't be hypnotized against your will, even by yourself. Entering a trance-like state during self-hypnosis is only possible if you are willing to relax deeply and open yourself to being hypnotized. You are never out of control.

However, during a state of hypnosis, you are more receptive to messages, which is precisely why it works so well for integrating positive beliefs that are easier to dismiss in a normal state. Therefore, I suggest doing self-hypnosis rather than going to a hypnosis practitioner, especially if you're scared. Our brains try to survive at all costs, and your brain protects you from harm. Getting stuck in a hypnotic state is a myth. You can try this self-hypnosis experiment fully confident that you will go in and out of hypnosis at exactly the right time.

Do's and Don'ts

- Self-hypnosis isn't complicated, but it does take practice. Be patient with yourself.
- Focus on one thing at a time. Don't list a litany of items you want to process or address during one session.
- Make sure you are undisturbed and comfortable, as the first step is deep relaxation.

Have fun with this and experiment. It's not a weird Vegas trick that will make you jump on one foot and cluck like a chicken. It's just a way to relax so deeply that your brain can integrate positive messages more easily.

NATURE

One of my favorite activities is skiing. I love flying down a mountain by myself, hearing only the wind. Taking in the majestic mountains, snow-covered trees, icy rivers and mountain lakes, and the clear blue sky gives me peace and happiness. My wife likes skiing but *loves* mountain climbing. Whether you enjoy nature from your hammock while reading a good book under the dappled shade of trees or feel the sun on your back while scaling a cliff, nature is good for us.

Much has been written on the positive effect of green spaces on our cognition, mood, mental health, and emotional well-being. A 2020 article by Kirsten Weir published in the journal *Monitor on Psychology* by the American Psychological Association suggests the same is true for blue spaces—aquatic environments such as rivers, lakes, and oceans.[60] The imagery and sounds of nature can

---

60 Weir, "Nurtured by Nature," 55-56.

recharge our brain and help us perform better on cognitive tasks, likely because they reduce stress and restore attention.

Specifically regarding happiness, "contact with nature is associated with increases in happiness, subjective well-being, positive affect, positive social interactions and a sense of meaning and purpose in life, as well as decreases in mental distress."[61]

More time in nature that feels remote and boasts high levels of biodiversity in plants and wildlife are consistently rated higher and produce more positive outcomes. However, even small breaks in urban parks, a view of a garden or terrace, or a quick walk can make a big difference. In other words, don't wait for the weekend to plan a backpacking trip into the wilderness. Start with small changes by adding plants to your living space or eating your lunch out in the sun today and see how it feels.

RELATIONSHIPS

One of the most important factors in human happiness is social interaction and connection. If you take only one insight from this book that has accumulated solid research evidence and is almost universally true for everyone, it is that close relationships increase happiness.

Mehl et al. looked at the difference in happiness between people who were less social and had more superficial conversations and people who were very social and had more intimate conversations. They concluded that the latter were happier and that "the happy life is social rather than solitary."[62] The longitudinal Harvard Study of Adult Development has documented the connection between participants' personality, life choices, and behaviors, and

---

61 Weir, "Nurtured by Nature," 53.
62 Mehl et al., "Eavesdropping on Happiness," 540.

their subjective well-being and health since the 1930s.[63] The study shows that a long, stable romantic relationship is one of the strongest predictors of happiness in later life. Most important is relationship satisfaction—not only whether you love your partner but also whether you like them and their company.[64]

ROMANTIC RELATIONSHIPS

Romantic relationships take a lot of effort, so choosing someone worth that investment is essential. Culturally, we believe in soul mates, but in reality, loving relationships are built on mutual respect, communication, compromise, and continually finding that middle ground. Relationships are complicated, as evidenced by high divorce rates and dissatisfaction with our primary relationships.

And yet, if they're healthy, these relationships regularly top the list of what provides people with the most happiness throughout their lives. So even though falling in love is not entirely under our control and is undoubtedly heavily impacted by chemistry and biology, we *do* have a choice about how to handle our infatuation. Who do we want in our lives permanently, and who are we willing to commit to for life? Making a bad choice often results in many years of heartbreak, not just for the adults involved but especially for our children.

Although it is a decision that requires serious consideration, we must be prepared for hardships even if we choose someone who is an excellent match for us. Like my friend Roy, we must be willing to invest time and effort. He had a rough go for the first two years of his marriage. Instead of throwing in the towel, he

---

63 Massachusetts General Hospital and Harvard Medical School, "Harvard Second Generation Study."
64 Waldinger and Schulz, "What's Love," 422–431.

started reading books and going to couple's therapy with his wife. Some marriages and relationships can't be saved with effort, but many can.

The book *The Five Love Languages* by Gary Chapman has been a beneficial resource for me to understand that all my relationships with people I love can be improved by understanding how they want to be loved. It is critical to love people how they are most comfortable receiving love, not how we are most comfortable giving it.

Finally, it's essential to see your life partner as a boyfriend and girlfriend, no matter how long you've been married or living together. Relationships are living organisms, and consistent attention breathes life into what will otherwise die.

By the way, Roy and his wife are still going strong eight years later and are currently expecting their third child together.

Parenting

For many of us, family ranks high on our priority list, yet we're also unsure how to create a happy family life. We often blame our parents for what we believe they did wrong in raising us. We rarely appreciate how hard parenting is until we do it ourselves. This doesn't mean parents never make mistakes, but most of us try our best in our familial and cultural contexts. I don't think it's helpful to try giving my kids what I didn't get growing up, materially speaking. But I do try to provide them with the tools, knowledge, time, and attention I wish I'd received when I was a kid.

Although parenting is difficult and complex, it's worth the effort because it has the power to set our children up for happiness later in life. One study by Waldinger and Schulz showed that "warmer relationships with parents in childhood predict greater security of attachment to intimate partners in late life," explaining that the findings "underscore the far-reaching influence of childhood environment on well-being in adulthood."[65]

I believe in the idea of quality over quantity. With that in mind, I make it count when I spend time with my kids. I eliminate distractions so that I can be fully present. I turn off my phone, and we don't just sit next to each other watching TV. It's important to me that I interact with my kids and listen attentively when they tell me about themselves, their experiences, and their ideas. My kids are still little, so we invent stories, listen to music, and sing and dance together. I let them lead and follow along, giving them my full attention. I try to embody a quote in one of my kids' favorite movies, *Kung Fu Panda*. Master Oogway says, "Yesterday is history, tomorrow is a mystery, and today is a gift. That is why it is called the present."

Although I actively try to model being present, one major issue in our family (and every other family I know) is figuring out how to deal with screen time and social media. We can teach our kids to take their lives back from their phones by example. This includes their time, attention, and privacy. Many resources can help with this, like app timers to restrict phone usage to a specific time frame. We can also completely remove certain apps from our phone, silence notifications, or establish phone-free dinnertimes and family activities. Much research suggests that social connection directly relates to positive psychological outcomes and well-being and that "young people who live virtually experience a compulsion to dissociate from real living, which causes emotional imbalances in family relationships."[66]

---

[65] Waldinger and Schulz, "Long Reach," 1443.
[66] Graciyal and Viswam, "Happiness or Pleasure," 104.

There are multiple ways to safeguard our privacy and personal data, such as ensuring tight privacy settings, secure connections, opting out of ad tracking, or using a virtual private network (VPN).[67] If your kids (or you) are already hooked on phones and other devices, don't be surprised if this isn't an easy transition. Less screen time can result in withdrawal symptoms and deep cravings. But with time, you'll be able to relax into the moment and be more fully present with loved ones. And if your kids aren't hooked on phones yet, you can help them establish good habits to begin with.

FRIENDSHIPS

You've probably heard the story about throwing a bunch of crabs in a box and seeing if they can escape. Watching the crabs, you'll soon realize that they're out only for themselves, trying to use one another to climb over and out of the box. Because they're not working together, no crab ever makes it out. Instead, they all drag each other down, over and over again. Don't be a crab, and don't befriend crabs!

We may have a lot of acquaintances we call friends, but how many people do we have in our lives whom we trust explicitly? Those are the friendships worth the investment of our time and effort. When I consider the people I want to be friends with, I think of whether they add anything to my life or take away from it. Do they expand my world or limit it? Do they lift me up or drag me down? Of course, to be worthy of good friends, I must be that kind of friend myself. I strive to add positively to my friends' lives.

---

67 Mark Milian, "5 Tips."

Once we have jobs, marriages, families, or all three, finding and maintaining friends can be tricky. However, true friendships are worth the effort and time, as they make us happier.[68] It's important to note that the study by Demir and Weitekamp found that the quality of our friendships and satisfaction with the relationship are more important than the number of friends we have.

Happiness can even have a contagious effect throughout our social and friendship networks. Nicholas Christakis, a researcher and professor who co-authored a Harvard Medical School study, found that "happiness is also a collective phenomenon that spreads through social networks like an emotional contagion."[69] The study looked at 5,000 people over the course of twenty years and found that "one person's happiness triggers a chain reaction that benefits not only their friends, but their friends' friends, and their friends' friends' friends. The effect lasts for up to one year. The flip side, interestingly, is not the case: Sadness does not spread through social networks as robustly as happiness. Happiness appears to love company more so than misery."[70]

I went to boarding school for a while during my high school years. I lived, ate, studied, and even bunked with many boys, some of whom became close friends. Our friendship has survived the decades, distance, and the different paths our lives have taken. We may not see each other for five years at a time, but when we do, it's like we never left. We fall back into our comfortable, close dynamic because the depth we cultivated so many years ago is still there. These are the friendships worth protecting and nurturing regardless of how busy our lives get.

---

68 Demir and Weitekamp, "I Am So Happy," 181–211.
69 Cameron, "Having Happy Friends."
70 Cameron, "Having Happy Friends."

WORK

Work encompasses our professional careers, financial situation, education and expertise, passion, and legacy. It's a significant predictor of happiness because we spend so much time at work.

My professor Ashish Nanda asked my fellow students and me to complete an exercise while studying at Harvard Business School. We divided a sheet of paper into two columns. On the left, we ranked our top ten priorities in life (education, family, money, travel, self-improvement, and so on). Then we estimated as honestly as possible how much time we spent on each priority every week and noted it in the right column. My classmates and I were shocked at how little alignment there was between our stated values and the time we dedicated to pursuing these priorities. For example, I listed family as my top priority, but it ranked only fourth based on my allocated time.

Professor Nanda talked about work-life balance and the importance of having more than just a career in our lives. I took his comments to heart and reflected on them for a few days. I came away with an unexpected conclusion: I didn't believe in work-life balance. I agreed with him that to live a full life, I wanted more than work and money, but I didn't believe that had to be true for everyone.

Before that point, work-life balance had always sounded like a utopian ideal we should all strive for to be happy. But now, I felt frustrated with this one-size-fits-all approach and the expectation it placed on us to manage this precarious balance. For so many of us, it is simply not achievable. If you work a regular full-time job, you likely spend more time on work than anything else on your list, with few options to drastically change this. Shaming people for not spending more time with their families when they have to work full time or more to provide for them isn't helpful. There are simply not enough hours in the day. Quitting a job or going part time to spend more time with the family is not an option if that means the bills won't get paid to keep that family housed and fed. I have little patience for these idealistic, generalized theoretical concepts that can't be realistically applied to day-to-day life.

WORK-LIFE HARMONY

I suggest that instead of work-life balance, you consider work-life harmony.

Often in life, balance is simply not achievable. Frequently, our circumstances require an extreme or skewed effort in one aspect of our lives or another. So, for me, the idea of work-life balance has never quite encompassed the complexity of life.

Work-life harmony includes accepting our unique circumstances and knowing what we are doing with our time and why. Instead of a one-to-one match of priorities and time spent, it is an approach to ensure our efforts align with our values. Working two jobs for a while to ensure our elderly parents are financially taken care of might be the best way to prioritize family. We may decide to stop working as many hours in an effort to get promoted once we reach a certain income level. Instead, we will spend that time coaching our kids' sports teams, traveling, or fly-fishing, understanding that this may require setting spending limits. On the other hand, if you are ambitious (or at an ambitious stage of your life) and want to double down on your career, go for it!

There is no wrong or right way to create a life. We're all different in what drives us and what we consider a meaningful use of our time. It all comes down to brutal honesty, self-awareness, and taking responsibility for our choices. What do we want our lives to look like when we're not worried about what others think of our priorities and values?

Perfectly balancing an entire life is impossible, and allotting our time in socially acceptable or trendy ways will lead to resentment and disappointment. Instead, we must dig deep to figure out the few things we consider worth our effort and finite time.

EXERCISE
Work-Life Harmony

Let's adapt the work-life balance exercise I explained in the previous section. Divide a sheet of paper into two columns and list your top ten priorities on the left. Now, instead of estimating your allotted time spent on each of these priorities on a daily basis in the right column, make notes about each of the ten priorities. For example, if you picked family, write down what immediately comes to your mind, such as:

- I don't know how to talk to my wife anymore.
- I only go to family celebrations because I feel obligated to do so.
- *I never have any time for myself away from my kids.*

Pay attention to your thoughts and feelings as you complete this exercise. Do you experience feelings of regret or resentment bubbling up? Work your way back to figure out the ideas that preceded the emotions. Maybe you're a woman with career ambitions who wants to spend more time on work for the next five years, but your partner is pressuring you to start a family. Maybe you have lost touch with friends and given up painting because you're a single dad, entirely focused on your children and nothing else. Perhaps you're ready to retire, but you're worried about whether your partner will accept the reduction in income and potentially lower economic status.

It is essential to make sure your priorities are yours and not someone else's. After reflecting on your original values, you may feel the need to reorder them or eliminate some in favor of new ones. Rather than simply identifying how much time you spend on what, figure out whether your life's effort is aligned with your most important values.

Which changes do you need to make? Where do you need to spend more or less time? Which priorities have you neglected or overemphasized? What hard conversation might you need to have with partners, bosses, or family members?

CAREER FULFILLMENT

In recent years, many people appear to have shifted from doing work they love and find meaningful to doing the least amount of actual labor while making the most money possible. And then the pandemic hit. It seems the movement of finding purpose in our work has been revitalized by our collective reflection on what makes a meaningful life. Social media has hyped and polarized the value of money. I believe money is a means to an end, not the goal itself. Of course, we need money to cover our basic needs like food, shelter, and clothing, but money needs to have a purpose beyond merely serving as a status symbol. You may think more money equals more happiness, but I believe it's much more important to do what you love, rather than what brings you the most money.

As the annual *World Happiness Report* found in 2022, we seem to be experiencing a shift toward "interest in new and subjective measures of well-being and a waning focus on income and production."[71] The COVID-19 pandemic appears to have heavily

---

71 Helliwell et al., *World Happiness Report: 2022*, 57.

influenced these changing ideas. Although the pandemic initially caused massive job losses (20 million in the United States alone in the early days of the pandemic), the labor market recovered rapidly. The volume of job openings surged, but employers had difficulty finding and retaining workers. Employees quit and switched jobs at record numbers (up to four times in 2021), with the *quit rate* reaching a twenty-year high in November 2021.

The Pew Research Center found that "those who quit and are now employed elsewhere are more likely than not to say their current job has better pay, more opportunities for advancement and more work-life balance and flexibility."[72] Considering that during the pandemic's Great Resignation, employees left primarily because of low pay, lack of advancement opportunities, and feeling disrespected at work, these statistics are encouraging. The researchers found that over half of these workers "see their current work situation as an improvement over their most recent job."

As previously discussed, money impacts our happiness only to a certain point, after which there are diminishing returns. Doing what we love can bring us joy continually. As Confucius said, "Choose a job you love, and you will never have to work a day in your life." Do what you love, and the income will follow. It may sound a little simplistic, but I genuinely believe that the happier you are, the better you will perform. The better you perform, the better opportunities will come your way. It will become a self-perpetuating cycle. Whether you are an artist, a lawyer, or a baker, we are attracted to people who are passionate about what they do.

In fact, a 2012 study by De Neve and Oswald found that happier people are more likely to get a college degree, be hired for a job,

---

[72] Parker and Menasce Horowitz, "Majority of Workers."

receive a promotion at work, and earn greater wealth throughout their lifetimes.[73] It's a two-way street. Money does make us happier, but being happier also results in higher earnings potential.

If you don't do what you love for work, being happy will be much more difficult, much like running an uphill marathon. If you find yourself in a situation where you can't quit an unfulfilling job and try something new, that's okay. You don't have to put in your notice immediately, but you *can* start working on your exit strategy. Use your free time to cultivate and learn the skills you need to succeed in a field you believe will make you happier. Yes, you do have free time. Maybe not very much, but there will be some in your day. It may mean less Netflix or scrolling on Instagram. Although there may be periods, even years, of working within extremely tight schedules, often we all have a few hours at night that we can use to prepare ourselves for taking the next step.

DOES MONEY MAKE US HAPPY?

It depends. The research I've shared in previous chapters of this book does show that more money increases overall life satisfaction, although it has little effect on our day-to-day feelings of happiness beyond that average $75,000 (or $90,000 when adjusted for inflation) per year mark. Even though there's a significant difference between the original and inflation-adjusted income, the general idea is that fulfilling our basic needs and attaining a measure of financial security does make us happier on a day-to-day basis. Beyond that, more money does give us higher life satisfaction when looking back. Of course, this could be caused by our need to compare ourselves to others, and if we feel we've done better than our

---

[73] De Neve and Oswald, "Estimating the Influence," 19954–19957.

peers, we'll likely rate our life as happier. There is no need to judge ourselves for this, as it's based on our evolutionary need to jostle for status in a group. However, it is something to be aware of when we assess ourselves and our lives. Could we be happy with what we have right now if it wasn't for the constant need to compare ourselves to what our neighbors and connections on social media have?

However, money does impact our lives in many ways that can increase or decrease happiness. Self-determination, which is significantly affected by money, makes people happier. An interesting study about millionaires and their happiness levels confirmed that "wealth enables people to take greater control of their lives, by giving the wealthy greater autonomy over how they choose to spend their time," which correlates with greater life satisfaction.[74] Another interesting finding from this study is that earned income indicates higher happiness, while unearned wealth (such as from an inheritance) is associated with decreased happiness. Our commonsense intuition that anything hard-won and achieved through personal effort garners a higher personal appreciation and more positive feelings appears to be true. According to the study, this phenomenon is not only related to money but also to consumer products, services like therapy, or belonging to social groups and networks.

WHAT YOU SPEND YOUR MONEY ON CAN MAKE YOU HAPPY

A *Time* magazine article from 2015 reviews interesting research-backed ways to increase happiness by spending money purposefully. Eric Barker explains that across different domains, frequency beats intensity, suggesting to "buy many small pleasures rather

---

74 Donnelly et al., "Amount and Source of Wealth," 696.

than fewer large ones."[75] Additionally, spending money on experiences rather than stuff and delaying gratification or consumption makes us happier, too. For example, people are often happier looking forward to a vacation and remembering it via photos after the fact than while they're on the actual vacation. Anticipating that vacation or other future events makes us happy.

Spending money on other people is also a surefire way to increase your own happiness, as we'll discuss later in this chapter.

PERSONAL GROWTH

Learn something new every day. It's not just good for your brain and the longevity of your mental faculties, but it's also just plain fun. There is no way to learn and discover everything in a single lifetime, so you can be sure your curiosity will never be exhausted.

LEARNING

How we learn doesn't matter as long as we're actively seeking opportunities to explore. Personally, I love losing myself in books. They serve as a private refuge that helps me recenter myself. And, of course, they're a treasure trove for learning new things. But books are not for everyone. If you like to watch TV, pick a documentary about a new topic. Choose an audiobook or podcast and dive in. Go to a community event or take an adult education class.

If you're open and curious, small moments in daily life become opportunities for wonder and discovery. We can learn from our children, community members, and colleagues, from our own mistakes, memories, and life events. To make sure the discovery sticks, it's a good idea to take a few minutes to reflect by writing

---

75 Barker, "8 Ways."

about it. One great way to integrate new knowledge is to teach it to someone else, maybe your spouse, kids, or an interested friend.

Mihaly Csikszentmihalyi, one of the founders of positive psychology, proposed that we aren't the happiest when we're passively relaxing, but when we're passionately engrossed in an activity that holds our full attention and challenges our skills. He coined the term "flow" as "the state in which people are so involved in an activity that nothing else seems to matter; the experience itself is so enjoyable that people will do it even at great cost, for the sheer sake of doing it."[76] These activities can be of a physical or mental nature, with the most important aspect being the challenge, the stretching of abilities, and the "voluntary effort to accomplish something difficult and worthwhile."

DON'T AIM FOR THE EASY A

A 2019 study in *Nature Communications* also speaks to this voluntary stretching of our limits, especially in the context of our academic pursuits and education. The researchers' 85 percent rule for optimal learning explains that we should fail about 15 percent of the time to ensure we're challenged enough to keep it interesting but not so far out of our depth that we give up altogether.[77] This is the sweet spot of learning—one that isn't always supported in academic institutions where the focus is on grades rather than learning and progress.

GIVING

Giving is one of the biggest contributors to happiness, according to several studies across countries, cultures, social class, finances,

---

76 Csikszentmihalyi, *Flow*, 4.
77 Wilson et al., "Eighty-Five Percent Rule," 1–2.

and age.[78] The joy of giving is something inherently human that binds us all together. According to a study by Moll et al. published in the *Proceedings of the National Academy of Sciences*, "human altruism draws on general mammalian neural systems of reward, [and] social attachment."[79]

The "helper's high" was conceptualized in the 1980s to explain positive emotions after providing a service or kindness to someone else, similar to the "warm glow" theory[80] that includes physical changes such as an increase in body temperature. Originally an economic model, the warm glow theory states that "people feel pleasure when they spend money on others."[81] A 2006 study by Moll et al. framed giving as a pro-social act motivated by selfishness because our brains release oxytocin and endorphins, rewarding us with happiness in return for doing a good deed.[82]

Helliwell and his colleagues found when compiling the *World Happiness Report: 2022* that an encouraging positive change during the COVID-19 pandemic was "global upsurge in benevolence in 2021. This benevolence has provided notable support for the life evaluations of givers, receivers, and observers, who have been gratified to see their community's readiness to reach out to help each other in times of need. In every global region, there have been large increases in the proportion of people who give money to charity, help strangers, and do voluntary work in every global region. Altogether the global average of these three measures was up by a quarter in 2021, compared with before the

---

78 Dunn, Aknin, and Norton, "Prosocial Spending," 41–47.
79 Moll et al., "Human Fronto-mesolimbic Networks," 15626.
80 Andreoni, "Impure Altruism," 464.
81 Johnson, "How Generosity Changes Your Brain."
82 Moll et la., "Human Fronto-mesolimbic Networks."

pandemic."[83] The term "life evaluation"—rather than "daily positive affect" or "momentary happiness"—reminds us that we need both to be truly happy. Although the pandemic and its lingering effects have caused heartbreak and destruction, pulling together to help each other appears to have instilled the kind of life satisfaction that comes from living a meaningful life.

Social scientist Michael Norton designed experiments in Canada and Uganda proving that spending money on others makes us happy. He gave people a small amount of money and instructed one group to spend it on themselves and another group to spend it on others. The participants who spent the money on other people self-reported higher happiness levels. Norton illustrates the point that more than how much money we have, it matters what we do with it. He asks us to imagine winning $5 million. Whether we burn that pile of cash, spend it on a hot air balloon, or give it all to charity will significantly impact how we feel about both that money and ourselves.[84]

Luckily, you don't need to be wealthy to give because it's not just about money. Decades ago, MIT started a nonprofit business accelerator to support small and medium businesses in developing countries. The project's thesis is that one critical way to create wealth in a community is to generate well-paying jobs in a robust ecosystem of growing companies. I started volunteering in 2016, and it has been a gratifying experience to give my time and expertise.

This way of giving aligns with the resources I can spare (my time), my skills and expertise (business development), and my values (strengthening communities through job opportunities).

---

83 Helliwell et al., World Happiness Report: 2022, 7.
84 Raz and Norton, "Can Money Buy You Happiness?"

You may be passionate about animal welfare, affordable housing, cancer research, mental health access, or child hunger. There are many worthy causes and ways to contribute including donating your time, money, skills, and expertise. You can give locally in your community or support national or international nonprofits and charities. If you haven't yet figured out how you'd like to contribute, it's worth taking the time to do so. Being able to contribute meaningfully to the world has dramatically increased my happiness.

Making giving an integral part of workplace culture also seems to be an incredibly powerful approach to increasing happiness. A 2018 study in the journal *Emotion* by Chancellor et al. shows how pro-social acts of kindness and giving positively impact both the giver and receiver.[85]

Their experiment had a group of givers practice five acts of kindness for a group of receivers over four weeks. The study results show that both "Givers and Receivers mutually benefited in well-being in both the short-term (e.g., on weekly measures of competence and autonomy) and the long-term (e.g., Receivers became happier after two months, and Givers became less depressed and more satisfied with their lives and jobs)." The results also confirmed that receiving kindness inspires people to pay it forward, with receivers exhibiting 278 percent more pro-social behaviors than the individuals in the control group. The researchers concluded that everyday pro-sociality is "an unequivocally positive experience" and both "emotionally reinforcing and contagious."[86]

---

85 Chancellor et al., "Everyday Prosociality," 507–517.
86 Chancellor et al., "Everyday Prosociality," 507.

HOBBIES

Recently, my wife and I visited some friends in California, and the husband took me golfing. I had never golfed before and didn't have the faintest idea about the game. Many of my friends are quite a bit older than me, and golfing is a favorite hobby in that circle. Our friend Harpreet taught me the basics and even helped me pick out my first set of golf clubs. It was a pain to take them back home on the plane and through security—talk about a bulky, awkward piece of luggage! However, learning from a friend and investing in the equipment, along with my wife's support to try something new, helped me overcome that initial fear of getting out of my comfort zone. Now I have a new skill to practice that offers me a way to exercise, while networking for my business with many colleagues who've enjoyed golf for years.

We may think we're too busy for hobbies, but they serve an essential function in our lives, combining the joy of learning something new with a socializing aspect. Whether reading, painting, skiing, or gardening, learning a new skill is good for our brains, and doing it with friends or making new ones in the process increases happiness-inducing social interactions. One 2017 study showed that adult education classes "enhanced well-being by improving mood and providing a sense of belonging. The classes helped participants develop self-confidence, create and strengthen relationships, and encouraged more active lives. Participants valued meeting people from their community and used these ties to access information about local opportunities."[87] Plus, many hobbies can also reduce stress and improve our physical and mental health. The meditative, stress-reducing nature of

---

87 Pearce, "Participants' Perspectives," 42.

hobbies like coloring, gardening, or yoga can provide a mental break, while physically active pursuits, such as individual and team sports, improve overall health.

Many hobbies don't require costly equipment, and most communities offer free or affordable events, lectures, classes, and activity groups. If there's something you've wanted to try out, I hope you do it. Sign up for that class! Ask a friend to teach you the basics. Give anything new a few tries so you can determine if it's up your alley or not.

PURPOSE

Whether you consider yourself spiritual, religious, or neither, the research on whether faith makes us happier is exciting and open to interpretation. A 2019 study from the Pew Research Center shows that actively religious people are, in fact, happier.[88] It's unclear if this is simply due to the faith itself or because religion often involves attending worship services and community involvement, which foster belonging and connection. In other words, it may be regular connections with people we trust and a solid social network rather than the religion itself that makes us happy.

Researcher and author Catherine Sanderson confirmed the findings that religion makes us happier. She also explains that both optimism and high self-esteem make us happy. These two personality traits could be inherent to our nature but are also supported by religious teachings. The idea that God is in control, everything will work toward good in the end, and that we are valued and loved by an omnipotent creator could understandably improve our self-esteem and optimism. Sanderson's research also

---

88 Marshall, "Religious People Happier, Healthier."

shows that the ability to take an adverse event and reframe it positively makes us happier. I think this may be easier for someone with religious or spiritual beliefs who looks at challenges and tragedies as a test or learning experience with a silver lining or crucial teaching moment.[89]

Of course, my ideas are mostly speculative and not exclusively applicable to believers versus nonbelievers. However, religious and spiritual practices do seem to give us many aspects of a happy life: connection with people, a higher purpose, and eternal certainty within temporal uncertainty.

If you're feeling a bit overwhelmed at this point by all the aspects of life that impact our happiness and have started to make a long list of things you must change, don't worry. You don't have to do everything at once.

EAT THE ELEPHANT PIECE BY PIECE

Theologian and activist Desmond Tutu said, "There is only one way to eat an elephant: a bite at a time." It's a good reminder that complex problems are best solved piece by piece, step by step.

Overhauling our entire lives is complex and overwhelming. Some of the advice in this chapter may resonate with you, and some may not. The critical thing to remember is that all of the areas of life discussed here add to your overall happiness. Nobody can confront all of these areas at once. You can start with the area lacking the most or choose one that feels the most accessible to you. You can choose the one you're most excited about confronting, the one most likely to bring the highest reward or deepest joy, or the one you're most scared of.

[89] Sanderson, *The Positive Shift*.

Setting self-concordant goals has been shown to increase well-being.[90] Self-concordant or self-congruent goals align with our values and identity and are born from our intrinsic motivation, rather than external factors. In other words, choosing meaningful goals autonomously and working toward reaching them makes us happy. Setting goals because of what we think is expected of us, even if it doesn't fit what we genuinely want to accomplish, doesn't have the same effect. Reaching goals alone doesn't make us happy. We must pick the right goals first.

One way to eat the elephant and make meaningful changes in your life is to set SMART goals.[91] This helpful acronym is a good reminder of how to set realistic goals that empower rather than sabotage our efforts.

S - PECIFIC

Being as precise as possible makes your goals concrete, rather than vague and ambiguous. Setting a goal of "meditating for ten minutes daily" is much more specific than "reducing stress." It's much easier to plan specific activities to reach these goals and to hold yourself accountable when you don't follow through.

M - EASURABLE

If you can't measure your progress while working toward a goal, you're much more likely to give up before reaching your objective. This is where you divide the elephant up into pieces and start chewing on the first one. For example, if you want to start a business, you'll need to come up with a name, register your company, get a tax ID, and so on. Checking off items on your list will

---

90 Deci and Ryan, "The 'What' and 'Why' of Goal Pursuits," 227–268.
91 Fournier, "Eat an Elephant."

provide a touchpoint for where you are in the process and keep you engaged and excited to continue.

A - TTAINABLE

Make your goals realistic to avoid self-sabotage and disappointment. If you haven't gone for a run since high school, don't sign up for a marathon next year. Start with a 5K and work your way up. Setting achievable goals may seem less exciting than shooting for the moon. However, you'll make more progress overall by completing them and building from there than you will from setting too ambitious of a goal, failing, and being too disappointed to start again.

R - ELEVANT

Setting goals you are passionate about and truly want to achieve is necessary for sticking with them through the inevitable challenges, slumps, plateaus, and temporary failures. Choosing a goal relevant to you is similar to choosing self-concordant or self-congruent goals. Because it takes hard work to reach a goal, you're more likely to succeed if you are deeply invested in the outcome.

T - IME-BOUND

Setting reasonable timelines for your goals keeps you accountable and progressing through the many steps necessary to accomplish an objective. You've probably heard the old saying, also known as Parkinson's law, that the work fills the time you allot for its completion. This doesn't mean you should set an unrealistically short time frame for your goal. However, keep in mind that if we give ourselves no deadline at all, we tend to procrastinate getting to work on our goals.

> **KEY TAKEAWAYS**
>
> - There is no single right way to live a life—reflect on what is important to you and what kind of life you want to lead (Exercise: Work-Life Harmony).
> - Identify the areas of your life that you need to change or improve.
> - Eat the elephant piece by piece.

We are complex people with complicated lives. There is no right order or correct way to make changes, but if you take time to reflect, you will know what is most relevant to your life and happiness right now. Start with one thing you can do today.

When this step-by-step process inevitably takes longer than anticipated, I practice self-compassion. Loving ourselves is an essential step on our journey to happiness.

Chapter 7

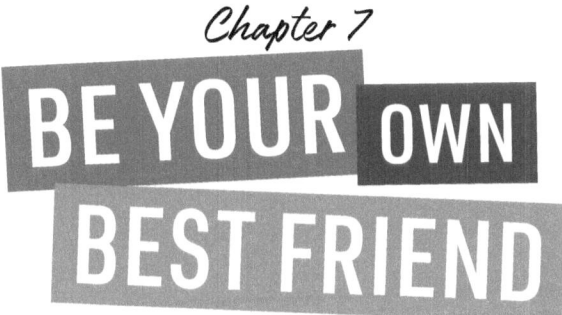
BE YOUR OWN BEST FRIEND

> The greatest gift you can give to others is the gift
> of unconditional love and acceptance.
> **—BRIAN TRACY, SPEAKER**

I visited Hawaii for the first time with my family when I was thirteen. I was big into volcanoes at that age, and seeing a lava river in real life blew my middle school mind. I could not believe I was in a place that combined volcanoes, jungles, waterfalls, and cities into an intoxicating, awe-inspiring experience of a lifetime. But although the natural beauty was astounding, I found something even more precious in a gift shop that I've carried with me to this day. In that small souvenir shop, I saw the Polynesian phrase *Ho'oponopono* and asked the store employee what it meant.

That's how I first learned about this ancient Hawaiian prayer and practice for reconciliation. There is no direct translation for the mantra, but it approximates "to make right" or "to make good." The four parts of this reconciliation practice are repentance, forgiveness, gratitude, and love. Whereas in traditional Hawaiian culture, the prayer informs rituals among families and communities, I use it quietly for myself, repeating in my head, "I'm sorry. Please forgive me. Thank you. I love you."

At thirteen, it was a practice that gave me peace amid the typical angst and chaos of early teenagerhood. I regularly felt insecure about my looks and body, my relationships with friends and family, and my worries about the future. As for many teenagers, it was difficult for me to identify and express my emotions. I was rarely mature enough to admit mistakes or ask for forgiveness from my parents or friends when I made a mistake. Ho'oponopono brought me calm by practicing loving and forgiving myself privately, which gave me peace and closure even if I had no control over the situation. One reason it affects an internal change is accepting full responsibility for one's actions, even if (in my case) it's never communicated to anyone else.

I still use Ho'oponopono today, especially in difficult circumstances that cause an onslaught of negative thoughts where I can't confront a person or situation directly, when I don't have the necessary tools, or I'm simply not ready. Dealing with any guilt or shame internally first often gives me the resolve and calm I need to eventually address the issue with other people.

I have found Ho'oponopono to be a powerful practice for dealing with past regrets and increasing my self-love. I often use this powerful mantra to remind myself that I need to extend all of the kindness I offer to others to myself as well. I need to forgive myself as much as I need to forgive others. This beautiful concept of reconciliation, restitution, and restoration helps me find peace and put the past to rest. It's not that important how you define forgiveness, only that you know what it means to you and that you extend it to yourself.

This chapter will dive into why it's vital for our happiness to love ourselves and how we can progress in that regard. Self-love comes in many flavors and names such as self-compassion, self-kindness, and self-acceptance. It can sometimes sound self-indulgent and egocentric, yet it is one of the essential practices to increase our happiness.

Associate Professor at the University of Texas at Austin Kristin Neff first popularized the term "self-compassion."[92] "Self-compassion entails three main components: (a) self-kindness—being kind and understanding toward oneself in instances of pain or failure rather than being harshly self-critical, (b) common humanity—perceiving one's experiences as part of the larger human experience rather than seeing them as separating and isolating, and (c) mindfulness—holding painful thoughts and feelings in balanced awareness rather than over-identifying with them. Self-compassion is an emotionally positive self-attitude that should protect against the negative consequences of self-judgment, isolation, and rumination (such as depression). Because of its non-evaluative and interconnected nature, it should also counter the tendencies towards narcissism, self-centeredness, and downward social comparison that have been associated with attempts to maintain self-esteem."[93]

WHAT ARE THE BENEFITS OF LEARNING SELF-COMPASSION?

- You will accept and forgive yourself.
- You will reclaim yourself and your life.
- You will love yourself and deepen your relationships.

---

92 Neff, "Self-Compassion," 85–101.
93 Neff, "Self-Compassion," 85.

ACCEPT YOURSELF

My friend Greg is among the happiest, most loving people I know. His favorite color is hot pink, and he loves wearing colorful outfits when he goes out dancing. He draws a lot of looks on the dance floor because he's got moves and wears eye-popping colors but also because he's very overweight.

We've been friends since we were nine years old. Greg was already a big kid then and was viciously bullied. Growing up, Greg wanted to become a DJ because he loved music, dancing, and flashy outfits. The DJ gig didn't work out, and he took a municipal job instead. However, he didn't lose his love for music, dancing, and glitzy clothes. Whether he's decked out in hot pink from his hat to his sneakers or rocking a bright red and neon yellow combo, he is unapologetically himself.

Greg knows the risk every time he goes out there. People may silently or openly make judgments about him. He may get dirty looks or even laughs. We're all humans concerned about our social standing. Being judged is difficult for anyone, but he loves himself enough to refuse to let mean-spirited strangers ruin his mood, his night out, or his self-acceptance. Greg is an inspiration to me, not because he doesn't care when people are cruel to him but because he refuses to give up on himself even in the face of cruelty. He will not wear drab clothes. He will not stay off the dance floor. He will not stop living his life and loving himself, no matter what other people think or say.

Disentangling ourselves from worrying about what others think of us is a lifelong process. Furthermore, other people's judgments can become intertwined with our own inner critic. Of course, it is healthy to acknowledge our faults and improve ourselves. However, it's not healthy to consistently tear ourselves down. When it comes to making decisions, we often have to disappoint ourselves or someone else. Greg has decided to have his own back and not disappoint himself by trying to fit into the box that others deem comfortable and appropriate for him.

Self-love grows out of self-acceptance. It is born of accepting our imperfect selves as we are in each moment. Accepting your true self doesn't mean you can't be different depending on the context of a situation or the people around you. It's normal to adapt to various situations by adjusting how we present ourselves, talk, dress, and act. Accepting your true self is much more about knowing who you are at your core and accepting what makes you uniquely you. Accepting our whole selves inspires positive change much more than being cruel and harsh. The voice in our head often sounds like a drill sergeant when what we need is the exact opposite. You've probably heard of the idea of treating and talking to ourselves like we'd speak to a friend we dearly love. It may feel strange at first, but it works.

Part of accepting ourselves is being nonjudgmental about the real limitations of our happiness.

EMBRACE THE LIMITATIONS OF YOUR HAPPINESS

I titled this book *The Happiness Practice* because I actively invest time and effort in happiness daily. I prefer the idea of practice over that of choice. Although I certainly choose to practice happiness daily, sometimes the idea that we can simply decide or choose to be happy doesn't consider the many limitations placed on our happiness. The aim of my personal journey and writing this book is not to say that we can all be perfectly happy all the time if we just make the decision. Instead, it is based on my deep belief that no matter our circumstances and background, we can be happier than we were in the past.

Just like we must be realistic about goal setting, we must be realistic about our happiness practice. Knowing and accepting our limitations may be painful at first, but it can also be liberating because it is an expression of the serenity prayer I've shared with you. It's another way of accepting what we can't change and focusing on what lies in our control.

BIOLOGICAL LIMITATIONS

Happiness researcher Sonja Lyubomirsky explains that people have a happiness set point, or a biologically and genetically determined predisposition for happiness.[94] This concept is also called the hedonic adaptation theory or hedonic treadmill, which explains that people tend to return to a baseline of happiness regardless of what happens in their lives. Earlier in the book, I've said that practicing happiness should never be used to shame people for not being happy enough, especially when dealing with mental health issues such as depression. The idea of a happiness set point underscores that accepting our biological baseline is the first step in accepting ourselves and making meaningful changes from that baseline.

The *World Happiness Report* puts the biological differences impacting happiness between people at 30–40 percent, with the remaining 60–70 percent a result of environmental influences.[95] According to Lyubomirsky, this happiness set point accounts for 50 percent of the difference in happiness among people. That sounds like a lot, I know. Another 10 percent are determined by external circumstances (which we'll talk about in a minute), and

---

94 Lyubomirsky, *The How of Happiness*, 48–62.
95 Helliwell et al., *World Happiness Report: 2022*, 10.

the remaining 40 percent are impacted by our thoughts, feelings, attitudes, and actions. That's quite a bit of wiggle room for making positive changes!

Even though the researchers can't quite agree on how much of our happiness is more or less fixed biologically, a significant percentage is flexible and just waiting for us to shape as we please.

GOVERNMENTAL AND SOCIETAL LIMITATIONS

I'm sure you've seen that annual list of happiest countries as part of the *World Happiness Report*. The ratings consider the GDP per capita, social support, life expectancy, corruption, freedom, and generosity. The most recent report lists the happiest countries as Finland, Denmark, Iceland, Switzerland, the Netherlands, Luxembourg, Sweden, Norway, Israel, and New Zealand.[96] You'll notice that neither the United States nor many other wealthy Western countries such as Canada or Germany made the top ten. And neither did my home country of Mexico.

The happiness of a country is not only related to financial wealth, of course; as with people, many interplaying conditions make up the big picture. Different studies have highlighted support for human rights, divorce rates, and political stability in addition to those surveyed by the *World Happiness Report*. One study showed that inclusive education policies can moderate the correlation between social background and happiness. In other words, coming from a lower social class has less of an impact on our happiness if we have access to education.[97]

Benjamin Radcliff, a political science professor at the University of Notre Dame, stated in a CNN interview that "happier

---

96 Helliwell et al., *World Happiness Report: 2022*, 17.
97 Högberg, "Educational Policies," 664–681.

people live in countries with a generous social safety net, or, more generally, countries whose governments 'tax and spend' at higher rates, reflecting the greater range of services and protections offered by the state...The more we supplement the cold efficiency of the market with interventions that reduce poverty, insecurity, and inequality, the more we improve quality of life for everyone."[98]

You may have heard of the happiness gap between parents and nonparents. Still, a study published in the *American Journal of Sociology* found an interesting explanation that has much less to do with having kids and much more to do with where you live while raising those kids. Jennifer Glass and her colleagues examined the effects of family policies in twenty-two countries. They found a "considerable variation in the parenthood gap in happiness across countries, with the United States showing the largest disadvantage of parenthood. The authors found that more generous family policies, particularly paid time off and child-care subsidies, are associated with smaller disparities in happiness between parents and nonparents."[99]

Unfavorable political and social circumstances, change, and turmoil, even in the service of a greater good, can also negatively affect our happiness. A study in the *European Journal of Political Economy* specifically focused on the happiness gap between post-socialist and advanced countries in Central and Eastern Europe and the former Soviet Union and found "increasing unhappiness that accompanied the transition process, including deteriorating public goods, rising inequality, income volatility, stagnating labor market conditions and changing norms."[100]

---

98   Radcliff, "Western Nations with Social Safety Net."
99   Glass, Simon, and Andersson, "Parenthood and Happiness," 886.
100 Nikolova, "Minding the Happiness Gap," 129.

However, this happiness gap has declined since the 1990s due to more political and institutional stability, macroeconomic factors, and the rule of law. In other words, at the country or government level, lots of change, uncertainty, and reforms, even if for the ultimate good, can make us unhappier, although the outcomes are better for our overall happiness.

All this is to say that the social, political, and cultural environments we grow up and live in impact our happiness to some degree. They are part of the 10 percent of outside circumstances that factor into our happiness level. It's essential to be aware of them without crediting them with too much influence.

DESPITE ALL THESE LIMITATIONS, LONG-TERM CHANGE IS POSSIBLE

One German study looked at long-term changes in happiness and life satisfaction over the course of seventeen years and found that it is, in fact, possible.[101] Although there was significant stability in happiness levels overall, nearly a quarter of participants reported a marked increase in happiness, and 9 percent showed a very substantial increase by two standard deviations or more.

Writer Seph Fontane Pennock cites a study by Barbara Fredrickson et al. that "showed that the stream of positive emotions induced through loving-kindness meditation can outpace the effects of the hedonic treadmill."[102] The researchers found that "loving-kindness meditation, a form of meditation that evokes feelings of warmth and care for oneself and others," doesn't just temporarily improve well-being but "reshapes enduring personality traits by helping us learn about the nature of our own minds"

---

101 Fujita and Diener, "Life Satisfaction Set Point," 158–164.
102 Fontane Pennock, "Hedonic Treadmill."

and "helps dismantle false assumptions about what leads to happiness and well-being."

PRACTICE SELF-KINDNESS THROUGH CHALLENGES

Swedish climate activist Greta Thunberg was diagnosed with Asperger's syndrome, OCD, and selective mutism. She describes what others may only see as mental illnesses as her superpowers. She says her OCD helps her stick to her convictions, like refusing plane travel to reduce her carbon footprint and instead crossing the Atlantic on a boat. Her Asperger's allows her to tell the truth without being too worried about hurting people's feelings. She permits herself to see these challenges not as a hindrance but as gifts to propel her forward on her path. Appreciating our challenges for what they can teach us and add to our lives, rather than taking away, and can be a powerful way to reframe our narrative.

Even without significant challenges, we all have strengths and weaknesses. As humans, we tend to focus on our mistakes and failures. What would happen if you instead looked at yourself from a strength-based perspective? We discussed in a previous chapter that kids live up to our expectations, good or bad. The same is true for us. If we expect ourselves to do well, we most likely will. If we focus on our strengths, they will expand. Our confidence will grow. The positive reinforcement will often prompt us to improve on an existing strength or work on a new one. Put down that heavy backpack. Try on kindness and self-compassion.

Treating ourselves with kindness is paramount when dealing with the old wounds and trauma that have a habit of popping up throughout our lives in disruptive ways. You may have heard about the Adverse Childhood Experience (ACE) study from the

Centers for Disease Control and Prevention (CDC) and insurance company Kaiser Permanente. The study surveyed more than 17,000 individuals on whether they had experienced one or more identified risk factors before age eighteen. These factors include physical, sexual, or emotional abuse, neglect, domestic violence, the loss or incarceration of a parent, or living with a family member who was grappling with substance abuse issues or mental illness.[103]

As a society, we sometimes belittle people who speak about difficult childhoods and how those experiences have shaped them. We often expect ourselves and each other to suck it up and get over it. However, in my own experience and marriage, I've found that it is much more helpful and healing to talk openly about the wounds and traumas from our childhoods. It has helped me immensely to learn about how some of my wife's behaviors and coping mechanisms originated from her childhood. Similarly, I've opened up to her about difficult times in my past. Humans are very resilient; many of us have probably experienced one or a few ACEs in our childhood and have been able to compensate quite well. However, the study showed that if the adverse experiences stack up, they can overwhelm children to the point of biological, emotional, and mental damage.

People with four ACEs or more can experience disrupted neurodevelopment and an increased risk for heart, lung, and liver disease and different types of cancers. They are more likely to struggle with emotional, cognitive, and social impairment such as becoming delinquent, experiencing homelessness, or underperforming at work. People with high ACE scores are more likely

---

[103] US Centers for Disease Control and Prevention, "CDC-Kaiser ACE Study."

to adopt high-risk behaviors such as smoking, alcoholism, and drug abuse and more often suffer from depression and suicidal ideation.

The truth is that deciding to be happy can't flip a switch and erase all our past wounds. However, a customized happiness practice, as explained in this book, including therapy, and based on self-kindness and acceptance can help you heal and improve your well-being.

UTILIZE POSITIVE SELF-TALK

Most of us live with an inner critic who relentlessly and harshly judges everything we do and say. It often feels like that critic is separate from us, but we need to remind ourselves that it is our own voice and that we have the power to change how we talk to ourselves. You've heard the suggestion to speak to ourselves as we would talk to a close friend. This thought exercise aims to remind us that we're worthy of the same kindness, love, and acceptance we extend to our friends. Even if it feels awkward initially, I've noticed that the more I pay attention to my internal dialogue, the less automatic it becomes and the easier it is for me to reframe harsh judgments into more neutral and accepting statements.

My friend Luis taught me how to use more affirming language by example. Whenever we see each other, he comments on something positive about me, whether it's my behavior, appearance, or a new skill. It's always something new, current, and true, regardless of how small the positive change is. He makes it a practice and a habit to actively look for the positive in others and then verbalize it. I now try to do the same with those around me, and it has significantly changed my constant internal chatter from negative or neutral to positive and uplifting.

As with many activities in this book, it's hard to tell what comes first. Often a behavior and its result reinforce each other to the point where it's hard to identify what came first. In this case, I have noticed that being aware of my negative self-talk and practicing positive, affirming language with others and myself have helped me stem the constant tide of internal criticism.

WHAT IF YOU DON'T BELIEVE YOU DESERVE LOVE?

I know I got lucky with loving parents and spiritual beliefs about a loving God, but I understand not everyone has had these experiences. If we have not been loved as children, it can be challenging to trust that we are lovable and worthy of kindness as adults. I don't want to dismiss the pain and challenge of this predicament, but I do want you to ask yourself, *Why not?* Why don't you believe you deserve love?

Identifying the false narratives surrounding our worthiness often helps us take the power and shame out of them and see ourselves in a more realistic light. We can address our feelings and thoughts about these opinions we've been taught as facts. This excavating work is difficult and painful but necessary to get to the bottom of our reasons for holding on to the belief of unworthiness.

At the end of the day, we are all flawed humans who are doing our best and deserve love and kindness.

EXERCISE
Two-Step Loving-Kindness Meditation

Loving-kindness meditations, or *metta*, the Pali word for "goodwill" or "loving kindness," can sometimes feel awkward or hollow when we don't believe that we deserve this intense loving attention and affection.

Step 1: Do You Deserve Love?
Before heading directly into the loving-kindness meditation, a few minutes of self-reflection may be beneficial. If you feel any resistance to speaking kind, loving words to yourself, you may secretly wonder if you deserve love. Maybe it is the engineer in me or my inner child asking a million *why?* questions, but this self-discovery could be the first step to change. Perhaps a parent, teacher, or partner has told you that you don't deserve love because of some perceived character defect, flaw in your appearance, personality trait, or a decision you made in the past.

Take a few minutes to write down where these feelings originated, the stories you've been told, and whose voice you're hearing in your head. *Are these stories true? Would you speak like that to a close friend? Even if some things are accurate or partially true, do they make you a bad person or unworthy of love?*

Once you've identified why you feel unworthy of love and whose voice is in your head, you can start questioning that narrative. This is likely not a one-and-done exercise, but starting to challenge your long-held beliefs about yourself can help lower your resistance to being open to a loving-kindness meditation practice.

Step 2: Loving-Kindness Meditation
Many meditation apps and YouTube channels offer free, guided loving-kindness meditations. You may listen to a guided meditation or repeat a mantra to yourself out loud such as the traditional:

May I be happy. May I be healthy. May I be at peace. May I be free.

You can also choose to direct metta at other people in your life or humanity as a whole and adapt the mantra accordingly:

May all beings everywhere be happy. May they be healthy. May they be at peace. May they be free.

You can experiment with metta by directing it at yourself or others. You can use it to increase feelings of love and gratitude for yourself or a loved one, use it as part of your grieving process or direct it at a person you have a complicated relationship with.

FIND YOUR SPIRITUAL CENTER

To reap its benefits, it's unnecessary to believe in any spiritual teachings associated with the loving-kindness meditation exercise. We can appreciate and utilize many practical teachings from various religious and faith traditions without subscribing to their totality. My Catholic faith helps me have a solid center, a deep well from which to draw. I believe that we are all made in God's image and worthy of love, but that's not the only reason to love ourselves.

I have many friends who belong to other faith traditions or none at all. I don't think it matters much what we believe in but that we believe in *something*. Even if you don't have faith in God, maybe you believe in the human spirit, in love, in kindness. This set of core beliefs gives us peace in an uncertain world where we cannot always find explanations for what is happening to us and those we love. Allowing ourselves this transcendent view of the world can make us more curious, rather than fearful, about the mysteries of life.

Whether you have any spiritual or religious beliefs, I think love is already present, and we can choose to dip into it or not. I don't believe love is something we have to generate but something that already exists and that we can decide to actively participate in or reject. Some of us might first feel it from loving parents, some from our belief in God, some through the kindness of a stranger, or the love of our children. Receiving love is as active as giving love. We must be open and vulnerable enough to receive love from others instead of closing ourselves off and rejecting the love. Giving love is also active as it's a behavior or a practice—a gift we extend to someone else that can, in turn, be received or rejected.

PRACTICE AND MODEL SELF-LOVE

When we don't love ourselves, it shows. We may lack the drive or ability to care for ourselves physically and emotionally. We may speak harshly about ourselves in front of others or be in relationships with people who put us down. We may be depressed and closed off.

We must be at peace with ourselves to help others and to be a steady, solid presence. This is most true when it comes to our kids. They are individuals, not mini versions of us. We must accept ourselves to truly accept our children for who they are.

Give your kids tools, not solutions. Whenever possible, I try to teach my kids how to figure problems out themselves. I can't fix everything for them for their entire lives, and I wouldn't want to even if I could. Instead, I want to guide them toward helpful tools and resources and instill a sense of confidence and capability in them to address their challenges head-on.

You can't wear out the phrase "I love you." Our kids need the same thing we all need—love. Don't go a day without telling them you love them. I make mistakes as a parent all the time, but I consistently express my love to my children. Every morning before school, I give my kids a pep talk about how much I love them and believe they will succeed at school. I always send them out the door with my encouragement and love. It's a small thing that I think can potentially make a massive impact on my kids.

A friend of mine once witnessed this routine and imagined two kids coming to school, one of mine and one from a family where they get no encouragement or are criticized before they go out into the world. How will each kid confront the day's challenges? How will they handle difficult assignments, fights with their best friend, insults from a bully, or getting in trouble with a teacher? He encouraged me to continue building up my kids before sending them out into the world every day. It meant a lot to me that my friend saw the value in my daily pep talks and I hope my kids will feel the same looking back on their childhood.

My love is not conditional or dependent on whether my kids behave well. I separate my love and encouragement from the fact that I have to discipline them occasionally or dole out consequences for unacceptable behavior. However, I never purposely withdraw love or affection as a punishment.

RECLAIM YOURSELF

Reclaiming yourself means reclaiming your purpose, time, and attention.

As I explained in a previous chapter, I went through a phase in college when I was partying and drinking a lot, not doing anything meaningful with my life. I wasn't putting in the effort required to succeed. I had mediocre grades and wasn't trying hard at anything.

I started devouring books and resources to help me identify and manage my priorities and time. Slowly, by eating the elephant piece by piece, I changed my life. I started practicing meditation to learn how to be comfortable in silence. Meditation taught me to be in my own company without succumbing to restlessness and the urge to find distractions. I took the mindfulness concept into my day, reminding myself to be present and notice the sounds, images, tastes, and textures all around me to ground me in the present. I turned off my phone more frequently, resulting in a calmer and quieter environment and a more tranquil mind.

No more self-sabotage. No more self-pity. No more self-loathing. Once I had decided to reclaim my life, I had to forgive myself for what I'd been doing, for wasting so much time. I had regrets about the past months, but I knew I needed to accept my previous choices to free myself to make new ones. I gave myself permission to move on, to begin again.

KEY TAKEAWAYS

- Accept and forgive yourself.
- Invest time and effort in your relationship with yourself.
- Practice positive self-talk.
- Focus on your strengths and gifts.
- Find a spiritual center inside yourself (Exercise: Two-Step Loving-Kindness Meditation).

It's not cheesy or weird to get intentional about the relationship you have with yourself. In fact, it's by far the most important work you can do because it positively impacts your life every day in every way. Your thoughts, feelings, relationships, decisions, and ultimately, your happiness are built on this foundation of self-love.

As Oscar Wilde said, "To love oneself is the beginning of a lifelong romance."

CONCLUSION

Dear friend,

Happiness doesn't choose you. You choose happiness. Every morning you wake up, you must decide again.

Today, I choose to practice happiness. Will you?

It is not easy, but then again, nothing worth having is easy. I have faith in you, and I know happiness is within your grasp. You can decide to change your life.

Although most of us strive to be happy, it sometimes sounds like it's a selfish endeavor, but research has shown the opposite. Being happy matters to life on this planet. As researcher and author Catherine Sanderson found, happy people are more helpful, loyal, and productive. In other words, happy people are not just healthier themselves but contribute to a better, more beautiful life for the people around them and humankind as a whole.[104]

In this book, I've chronicled the step-by-step journey I took to find my own way to happiness. I hope my path inspires you to forge your own. Some of the conclusions I've drawn and the resources and tools I've shared may be a perfect fit for your life, and some may not. Trust yourself to know what works for you, and discard the rest. And, of course, you can always experiment and add tools to your life by trial and error. I hope the exercises throughout the book have made theoretical concepts more practical and accessible. Knowledge alone isn't worth much unless you apply it to your life.

My hope for this book is that it becomes a resource guide for you, marked up, underlined, dog-eared, and shared with friends and family members. If I could ask you for just one small favor: please choose an activity, exercise, or resource that speaks to you, and try it out. As much as I appreciate that you have read about my journey, the objective of this book has always been to inspire you to join me in making happiness a practice.

The world is a complicated place filled with pain and struggle. Even the path forward is often littered with obstacles, some of our own making. Practicing happiness is not about ignoring the darkness. It is a conscious decision to accept the darkness while turning toward the light.

Be whole. Be yourself. Be happy.

In friendship,

Victor

PS: I would love to hear from you. If you've decided to try any of the suggestions in this book, I'd love to know how it went. What is your personal understanding of happiness, and how do you bring it into your life?

You can email me at practicehappinesstoday@gmail.com.

Let's start a worldwide conversation to raise our personal and collective happiness!

BIBLIOGRAPHY

Agteren, Joep van, Matthew Iasiello, Laura Lo, Jonathan Bartholomaeus, Zoe Kopsaftis, Marissa Carey, and Michael Kyrios. "A Systematic Review and Meta-analysis of Psychological Interventions to Improve Mental Wellbeing." *Nature Human Behaviour* 5, no. 5 (May 2021): 631–652. https://doi.org/10.1038/s41562-021-01093-w.

American Academy of Child and Adolescent Psychiatry. "Children and Divorce." AACAP.org. Last modified January 2017. https://www.aacap.org/AACAP/Families_and_Youth/Facts_for_Families/FFF-Guide/Children-and-Divorce-001.aspx.

Andreoni, James. "Impure Altruism and Donations to Public Goods: A Theory of Warm-Glow Giving." *The Economic Journal* 100, no. 401 (June 1990): 464–477. https://doi.org/10.2307/2234133.

Barker, Eric. "8 Ways That Money Can Buy Happiness." *Time*, February 12, 2015. https://time.com/3702054/how-money-can-buy-happiness/.

Basso, Julia C., and Wendy A. Suzuki. "The Effects of Acute Exercise on Mood, Cognition, Neurophysiology, and Neurochemical Pathways: A Review." *Brain Plasticity* 2, no. 2 (2017): 127–152. https://doi.org/10.3233/bpl-160040.

Ben-Shahar, Tal. *Happier: Learn the Secrets to Daily Joy and Lasting Fulfillment.* New York: McGraw-Hill, 2007.

Brown, Sara. "Social Media Is Broken. A New Report Offers 25 Ways to Fix It." *Ideas Made to Matter* (blog), MIT Sloan, June 30, 2021. https://mitsloan.mit.edu/ideas-made-to-matter/social-media-broken-a-new-report-offers-25-ways-to-fix-it.

Cameron, David. "Having Happy Friends Can Make You Happy." *The Harvard Gazette*, December 5, 2008. https://news.harvard.edu/gazette/story/2008/12/having-happy-friends-can-make-you-happy/.

Castaneda Aguilar, R. Andres, Tony Fujs, Christoph Lakner, Daniel Gerszon Mahler, Minh Cong Nguyen, and Samuel Kofi Tetteh Baah. "September 2020 Global Poverty Update from the World Bank: New Annual Poverty Estimates Using the Revised 2011 PPPS." *Data Blog*. World Bank Blogs, October 7, 2020. https://blogs.worldbank.org/opendata/september-2020-global-poverty-update-world-bank-new-annual-poverty-estimates-using-revised.

Chancellor, Joseph, Seth Margolis, Katherine Jacobs Bao, and Sonja Lyubomirsky. "Everyday Prosociality in the Workplace: The Reinforcing Benefits of Giving, Getting, and Glimpsing." *Emotion* 18, no. 4 (June 2018): 507–517. https://psycnet.apa.org/doiLanding?doi=10.1037%2Femo0000321.

Collier, Lorna. "Growth after Trauma." *Monitor on Psychology* 47, no. 10 (November 2016): 48. https://www.apa.org/monitor/2016/11/growth-trauma.

Covey, Stephen R. Foreword to *Lead or Get Off the Pot!: The Seven Secrets of a Self-Made Leader*, xiii–xvii. Pat Croce. New York: Fireside, 2004.

Csikszentmihalyi, Mihaly. *Flow: The Psychology of Optimal Experience*. New York: Harper and Row, 1990.

Davies, Jim. "New Evidence That Therapy Can Make You Happier." *Nautilus*, July 1, 2021. https://nautil.us/new-evidence-that-therapy-can-make-you-happier-238241.

Deci, Edward L., and Richard M. Ryan. "The 'What' and 'Why' of Goal Pursuits: Human Needs and the Self-Determination of Behavior." *Psychological Inquiry* 11, no. 4 (2000): 227–268. https://doi.org/10.1207/s15327965pli1104_01.

Decision Lab, The. "Why Do We Use Similarity to Gauge Statistical Probability? Where This Bias Occurs." Accessed June 10, 2022. https://thedecisionlab.com/biases/representativeness-heuristic.

Demır, Melıkşah, and Lesley A. Weitekamp. "I Am So Happy 'Cause Today I Found My Friend: Friendship and Personality as Predictors of Happiness." *Journal of Happiness Studies* 8, no. 2 (June 2007): 181–211. https://doi.org/10.1007/s10902-006-9012-7.

De Neve, Jan-Emmanuel, and Andrew J. Oswald. "Estimating the Influence of Life Satisfaction and Positive Affect on Later Income Using Sibling Fixed Effects." *Proceedings of the National Academy of Sciences* 109, no. 49 (December 2012): 19953–19958. https://doi.org/10.1073/pnas.1211437109.

Donnelly, Grant E., Tianyi Zheng, Emily Haisley, and Michael I Norton. "The Amount and Source of Millionaires' Wealth (Moderately) Predicts Their Happiness." *Personality and Social Psychology Bulletin* 44, no. 5 (May 2018): 684–699. https://doi.org/10.1177/0146167217744766.

Dunn, Elizabeth W., Lara B. Aknin, and Michael I. Norton. "Prosocial Spending and Happiness: Using Money to Benefit Others Pays Off." *Current Directions in Psychological Science* 23, no. 1 (February 2014): 41–47. https://doi.org/10.1177/0963721413512503.

Emmons, Robert A., and Michael E. McCullough. "Counting Blessings versus Burdens: An Experimental Investigation of Gratitude and Subjective Well-Being in Daily Life." *Journal of Personality and Social Psychology* 84, no. 2 (February 2003): 377–389. https://doi.org/10.1037//0022-3514.84.2.377.

Fontane Pennock, Seph. "The Hedonic Treadmill—Are We Forever Chasing Rainbows?" PositivePsychology.com, September 5, 2016. https://positivepsychology.com/hedonic-treadmill/.

Ford, Brett Q., Phoebe Lam, Oliver P. John, and Iris B. Mauss. "The Psychological Health Benefits of Accepting Negative Emotions and Thoughts: Laboratory, Diary, and Longitudinal Evidence." *Journal of Personality and Social Psychology* 115, no. 6 (December 2018): 1075–1092. https://doi.org/10.1037/pspp0000157.

Fournier, Denise. "The Only Way to Eat an Elephant." Psychology Today, April 24, 2018. https://www.psychologytoday.com/us/blog/mindfully-present-fully-alive/201804/the-only-way-eat-elephant.

Frankl, Viktor E. *Man's Search for Meaning*. Translated by Ilse Lasch. London: Rider, 2004.

Fujita, Frank, and Ed Diener. "Life Satisfaction Set Point: Stability and Change." *Journal of Personality and Social Psychology* 88, no. 1 (2005): 158–164. https://doi.org/10.1037/0022-3514.88.1.158.

Glass, Jennifer, Robin W. Simon, and Matthew A. Andersson. "Parenthood and Happiness: Effects of Work-Family Reconciliation Policies in 22 OECD Countries." *American Journal of Sociology* 122, no. 3 (November 2016): 886–929. https://doi.org/10.1086/688892.

Gordon, Amie M., Emily A. Impett, Aleksandr Kogan, Christopher Oveis, and Dacher Keltner. "To Have and to Hold: Gratitude Promotes Relationship Maintenance in Intimate Bonds." *Journal of Personality and Social Psychology* 103, no. 2 (2012): 257–274. https://doi.org/10.1037/a0028723.

Graciyal, D. Guna, and Deepa Viswam. "Social Media and Emotional Well-Being: Pursuit of Happiness or Pleasure." *Asia Pacific Media Educator* 31, no. 1 (June 2021): 99–115. https://doi.org/10.1177/1326365x211003737.

Grant, Kirsty. "Influencers React to Norway Photo Edit Law: 'Welcome Honesty' or a 'Shortcut'?" BBC News, July 6, 2021. https://www.bbc.com/news/newsbeat-57721080.

Hedgcock, William M., Andrea W. Luangrath, and Raelyn Webster. "Counterfactual Thinking and Facial Expressions among Olympic Medalists: A Conceptual Replication of Medvec, Madey, and Gilovich's (1995) Findings." *Journal of Experimental Psychology: General* 150, no. 6 (November 2020): e13–e21. https://doi.org/10.1037/xge0000992.

Helliwell, John F., Richard Layard, Jeffrey D. Sachs, Jan-Emmanuel De Neve, Lara B. Aknin, Shun Wang, and Sharon Paculor, eds. *World Happiness Report: 2022*. New York: Sustainable Development Solutions Network, 2022. https://worldhappiness.report/ed/2022/.

Högberg, Björn. "Educational Policies and Social Inequality in Well-Being among Young Adults." *British Journal of Sociology of Education* 40, no. 5 (2019): 664–681. https://doi.org/10.1080/01425692.2019.1576119.

Howell, Ryan T., David Chenot, Graham Hill, and Colleen J. Howell. "Momentary Happiness: The Role of Psychological Need Satisfaction." *Journal of Happiness Studies* 12, no. 1 (March 2011): 1–15. https://doi.org/10.1007/s10902-009-9166-1.

Hunt, Melissa G., Rachel Marx, Courtney Lipson, and Jordyn Young. "No More FOMO: Limiting Social Media Decreases Loneliness and Depression." *Journal of Social and Clinical Psychology* 37, no. 10 (December 2018): 751–768. https://doi.org/10.1521/jscp.2018.37.10.751.

Johnson, Stephen. "How Generosity Changes Your Brain." Big Think, September 30, 2021. https://bigthink.com/neuropsych/psychology-of-giving-to-charity.

Kahneman, Daniel, and Angus Deaton. "High Income Improves Evaluation of Life but Not Emotional Well-Being." *Proceedings of the National Academy of Sciences* 107, no. 38 (September 2010): 16489–16493. https://doi.org/10.1073/pnas.1011492107.

Kübler-Ross, Elisabeth. *On Death and Dying*. New York: Scribner Classics, 1997.

Lai, Jun S., Sarah Hiles, Alessandra Bisquera, Alexis J. Hure, Mark McEvoy, and John Attia. "A Systematic Review and Meta-analysis of Dietary Patterns and Depression in Community-Dwelling Adults." *The American Journal of Clinical Nutrition* 99, no. 1 (January 2014): 181–197. https://doi.org/10.3945/ajcn.113.069880.

Lawrence, Elizabeth M., Richard G. Rogers, and Tim Wadsworth. "Happiness and Longevity in the United States." *Social Science and Medicine* 145 (November 2015): 115–119. https://doi.org/10.1016/j.socscimed.2015.09.020.

Lucas, Michel, Fariba Mirzaei, An Pan, Olivia I. Okereke, Walter C. Willett, Éilis J. O'Reilly, Karestan Koenen, and Alberto Ascherio. "Coffee, Caffeine, and Risk of Depression among Women." *Archives of Internal Medicine* 171, no. 17 (2011): 1571–1578. https://doi.org/10.1001/archinternmed.2011.393.

Luft, Joseph. "The Johari Window: A Graphic Model of Awareness and Interpersonal Relations." *Human Relations Training News* 5, no. 1 (Spring 1961): 6–7. https://archive.org/details/sim_human-relations-training-news_spring-1961_5_1/page/6/mode/2up.

Lyubomirsky, Sonja. *The How of Happiness: A Scientific Approach to Getting the Life You Want.* New York: Penguin, 2008.

Magee, Elaine. "The Facts about Food Cravings." *Nourish* (blog). WebMD. Accessed October 26, 2022. https://www.webmd.com/diet/features/the-facts-about-food-cravings.

Manago, Adriana M., and Lanen Vaughn. "Social Media, Friendship, and Happiness in the Millennial Generation." Abstract. In *Friendship and Happiness: Across the Life-Span and Cultures*, edited by Melikşah Demir, 187–206. Dordrecht: Springer Science+Business Media, 2015. https://doi.org/10.1007/978-94-017-9603-3_11.

Marshall, Joey. "Are Religious People Happier, Healthier? Our New Global Study Explores This Question." Pew Research Center, January 31, 2019. https://www.pewresearch.org/fact-tank/2019/01/31/are-religious-people-happier-healthier-our-new-global-study-explores-this-question/.

Massachusetts General Hospital and Harvard Medical School. "Harvard Second Generation Study." Accessed July 5, 2022. https://www.adultdevelopmentstudy.org/.

Mehl, Matthias R., Simine Vazire, Shannon E. Holleran, and C. Shelby Clark. "Eavesdropping on Happiness: Well-Being Is Related to Having Less Small Talk and More Substantive Conversations." *Psychological Science* 21, no. 4 (April 2010): 539–541. https://doi.org/10.1177/0956797610362675.

Milian, Mark. "5 Tips for Controlling Your Privacy Online." CNN, December 13, 2010. http://edition.cnn.com/2010/TECH/web/12/13/5.online.privacy.tips/index.html.

Moll, Jorge, Frank Krueger, Roland Zahn, Matteo Pardini, Ricardo de Oliveira-Souza, and Jordan Grafman. "Human Fronto-mesolimbic Networks Guide Decisions about Charitable Donation." *Proceedings of the National Academy of Sciences* 103, no. 42 (2006): 15623–15628. https://doi.org/10.1073/pnas.0604475103.

Neff, Kristin. "Self-Compassion: An Alternative Conceptualization of a Healthy Attitude toward Oneself." *Self and Identity* 2, no. 2 (2003): 85–101. https://doi.org/10.1080/15298860309032.

Nikolova, Milena. "Minding the Happiness Gap: Political Institutions and Perceived Quality of Life in Transition." *European Journal of Political Economy* 45, supplement (December 2016): 129–148. https://doi.org/10.1016/j.ejpoleco.2016.07.008.

Parker, Kim, and Juliana Menasce Horowitz. "Majority of Workers Who Quit a Job in 2021 Cite Low Pay, No Opportunities for Advancement, Feeling Disrespected." Pew Research Center, March 9, 2022. https://www.pewresearch.org/fact-tank/2022/03/09/majority-of-workers-who-quit-a-job-in-2021-cite-low-pay-no-opportunities-for-advancement-feeling-disrespected/.

Pearce, Eiluned. "Participants' Perspectives on the Social Bonding and Well-Being Effects of Creative Arts Adult Education Classes." *Arts and Health* 9, no. 1 (2017): 42–59. https://doi.org/10.1080/17533015.2016.1193550.

Princing, McKenna. "What You Need to Know about Toxic Positivity." *Right as Rain* (blog), UW Medicine, September 8, 2021. https://rightasrain.uwmedicine.org/mind/well-being/toxic-positivity.

Psychology Today. "Grief." Accessed October 26, 2022. https://www.psychologytoday.com/us/basics/grief.

Radcliff, Benjamin. "Western Nations with Social Safety Net Happier." CNN, September 25, 2013. https://www.cnn.com/2013/09/25/opinion/radcliff-politics-of-happiness/index.html.

Rao, Min, Xiaotian Wang, Hailong Sun, and Kun Gai. "Subjective Well-Being in Nostalgia: Effect and Mechanism." *Psychology* 9, no. 7 (July 2018): 1720–1730. https://doi.org/10.4236/psych.2018.97102.

Raz, Guy, and Michael Norton, "Can Money Buy You Happiness?" NPR, April 4, 2014. https://www.npr.org/transcripts/297888687.

Reber, Arthur S. *The Penguin Dictionary of Psychology*. 2nd ed. London: Penguin, 1995.

Rienks, J, A J Dobson, and G D Mishra. "Mediterranean Dietary Pattern and Prevalence and Incidence of Depressive Symptoms in Mid-Aged Women: Results from a Large Community-Based Prospective Study." *European Journal of Clinical Nutrition* 67, no. 1 (2012): 75–82. https://doi.org/10.1038/ejcn.2012.193.

Sanderson, Catherine Ashley. *The Positive Shift: Mastering Mindset to Improve Happiness, Health, and Longevity*. Dallas: BenBella Books, 2019.

Sauteraud, Alain. "The 'Stages of Grief' Do Not Exist." *Journal de thérapie comportementale et cognitive* 28, no. 2 (June 2018): 93–95. https://doi.org/10.1016/j.jtcc.2018.02.001.

Shiv, Baba. "Baba Shiv: How Do You Find Breakthrough Ideas?" Insights by Stanford Business, October 15, 2013. https://www.gsb.stanford.edu/insights/baba-shiv-how-do-you-find-breakthrough-ideas.

Smith, Elliot. "The Barings Collapse 25 Years On: What the Industry Learned after One Man Broke a Bank." CNBC, February 26, 2020. https://www.cnbc.com/2020/02/26/barings-collapse-25-years-on-what-the-industry-learned-after-one-man-broke-a-bank.html.

Statista Research Department. "Value of Per Capita Income across India from Financial Year 2011 to 2021." Statista, September 12, 2022. https://www.statista.com/statistics/935754/india-per-capita-income-value/.

Stellar, Jennifer E., Neha John-Henderson, Craig L. Anderson, Amie M. Gordon, Galen D. McNeil, and Dacher Keltner. "Positive Affect and Markers of Inflammation: Discrete Positive Emotions Predict Lower Levels of Inflammatory Cytokines." *Emotion* 15, no. 2 (April 2015): 129–133. https://doi.org/10.1037/emo0000033.

Suttie, Jill. "Why You Should Sleep Your Way to the Top." *Greater Good Magazine*, December 1, 2013. https://greatergood.berkeley.edu/article/item/why_sleep_your_way_top.

Tang, Nicole K. Y., Mark Fiecas, Esther F. Afolalu, and Dieter Wolke. "Changes in Sleep Duration, Quality, and Medication Use Are Prospectively Associated with Health and Well-Being: Analysis of the UK Household Longitudinal Study." *Sleep* 40, no. 3 (March 2017): zsw079. https://doi.org/10.1093/sleep/zsw079.

Tedeschi, Richard G. "Growth after Trauma." *Harvard Business Review*, July–August 2020. https://hbr.org/2020/07/growth-after-trauma.

US Centers for Disease Control and Prevention. "About the CDC–Kaiser ACE Study." National Center for Injury Prevention and Control, Division of Violence Prevention. Last modified April 6, 2021. https://www.cdc.gov/violenceprevention/aces/about.html.

US Centers for Disease Control and Prevention. "Teen Drivers." National Center for Injury Prevention and Control. Last modified May 14, 2021. https://www.cdc.gov/transportationsafety/teen_drivers/index.html.

Waldinger, Robert J., and Marc S. Schulz. "The Long Reach of Nurturing Family Environments: Links with Midlife Emotion-Regulatory Styles and Late-Life Security in Intimate Relationships." *Psychological Science* 27, no. 11 (November 2016): 1443–1450. https://doi.org/10.1177/0956797616661556.

Waldinger, Robert J., and Marc S. Schulz. "What's Love Got to Do with It? Social Functioning, Perceived Health, and Daily Happiness in Married Octogenarians." *Psychology and Aging* 25, no. 2 (June 2010): 422–431. https://doi.org/10.1037/a0019087.

Walker, Matthew. *Why We Sleep: Unlocking the Power of Sleep and Dreams.* New York: Scribner, 2017.

Weir, Kirsten. "Nurtured by Nature: Psychological Research Is Advancing Our Understanding of How Time in Nature Can Improve Our Mental Health and Sharpen Our Cognition." *Monitor on Psychology* 51, no. 3 (April/May 2020): 50–56. https://www.apa.org/monitor/2020/04/nurtured-nature.

Wilson, Robert C., Amitai Shenhav, Mark Straccia, and Jonathan D. Cohen. "The Eighty-Five Percent Rule for Optimal Learning." *Nature Communications* 10, no. 1, article 4646 (November 2019): 1–10. https://doi.org/10.1038/s41467-019-12552-4.

Wirtz, Derrick, Amanda Tucker, Chloe Briggs, and Alexander M. Schoemann. "How and Why Social Media Affect Subjective Well-Being: Multi-site Use and Social Comparison as Predictors of Change across Time." *Journal of Happiness Studies* 22, no. 4 (April 2021): 1673–1691. https://doi.org/10.1007/s10902-020-00291-z.

Zickerman, Adam, and Bill Schley. *Power of 10: The Once-a-Week Slow Motion Fitness Revolution.* New York: HarperCollins, 2003.

ABOUT THE AUTHOR

Victor Mena is an industrial engineer with a rich educational background, having studied at Harvard University, Stanford University, MIT, and the University of California, Berkeley. Passionate about understanding how perspective shapes our internal world and external interactions, Victor has supported loved ones in their journeys to face alcoholism, depression, divorce, and terminal illness. Victor practices happiness every day and enjoys traveling, skiing, and reading. He lives in Mexico with his wife and two children.

www.ingramcontent.com/pod-product-compliance
Lightning Source LLC
Chambersburg PA
CBHW060524080526
44586CB00012B/606